MAKING SENSE OF **HISTORY**

1901– PRESENT DAY

JOHN D. CLARE
NEIL BATES
ALEC FISHER
RICHARD KENNETT

DYNAMIC
LEARNING

HODDER
EDUCATION
AN HACHETTE UK COMPANY

The Schools History Project

Set up in 1972 to bring new life to history for students aged 13–16, the Schools History Project continues to play an innovatory role in secondary history education. From the start, SHP aimed to show how good history has an important contribution to make to the education of a young person. It does this by creating courses and materials which both respect the importance of up-to-date, well-researched history and provide enjoyable learning experiences for students.

Since 1978 the Project has been based at Trinity and All Saints University College Leeds. It continues to support, inspire and challenge teachers through the annual conference, regional courses and website: www.schoolshistoryproject.org.uk. The Project is also closely involved with government bodies and awarding bodies in the planning of courses for Key Stage 3, GCSE and A level.

Although every effort has been made to ensure that website addresses are correct at time of going to press, Hodder Education cannot be held responsible for the content of any website mentioned in this book. It is sometimes possible to find a relocated web page by typing in the address of the home page for a website in the URL window of your browser.

Hachette UK's policy is to use papers that are natural, renewable and recyclable products and made from wood grown in sustainable forests. The logging and manufacturing processes are expected to conform to the environmental regulations of the country of origin.

Orders: please contact Bookpoint Ltd, 130 Milton Park, Abingdon, Oxon OX14 4SB. Telephone: (44) 01235 827720. Fax: (44) 01235 400454. Email education@bookpoint.co.uk Lines are open from 9 a.m. to 5 p.m., Monday to Saturday, with a 24-hour message answering service. You can also order through our website: www.hoddereducation.co.uk

ISBN: 978 1 4718 0596 7

© John D. Clare, Alec Fisher, Neil Bates, Richard Kennett

First published in 2015 by

Hodder Education,

An Hachette UK Company

Carmelite House

50 Victoria Embankment

London EC4Y 0DZ

www.hoddereducation.co.uk

Impression number 10 9 8 7 6 5 4 3 2 1

Year   2019 2018 2017 2016 2015

Cover photo © Stocktrek Images, Inc. / Alamy

Illustrations by Barking Dog Art, Peter Lubach, Tony Randell and Oxford Designers and Illustrators

Design layouts by Lorraine Inglis Design

Typeset in PMN Caecilia Light 10/13pt

Printed in Italy

A catalogue record for this title is available from the British Library.

ISBN 978 1 4718 0596 7

Acknowledgements

Every effort has been made to trace all copyright holders, but if any have been inadvertently overlooked the Publishers will be pleased to make the necessary arrangements at the first opportunity. The Publishers would like to thank the following for permission to reproduce copyright material.

p.2 Fritz Bilfinger, telegram dated 30 August 1945, copy, ICRC Archives, file No. G. 8/76; **p.11** Quote used with permission of Max Hastings; **p.11** Quote used with permission of Gerhard Hirschfeld; **p.11** Quote used with permission of Richard Evans; **p.29** 'These hands' song by The Wakes. Used by permission from The Wakes; **p.44** The British historian, journalist and Second World War expert Andrew Roberts, speaking to HistoryNet in 2011; **p.72** Edith Milner, writing in *The Times*, 29 October 1906; **p.81** 'The Ghost of the cable street' song by The Men they couldn't hang; **p.85** © Guardian News & Media Ltd. 2015; **p.86** Quote from Arthur Scargill, TV interview on *Good Morning Britain*, August 1984; **p.90** An internet comment by a member of the public calling himself 'Noel's Barmy Army', May 2005; **p.91** Five short poems without titles. Written for a BBC2 documentary December 1985'', reprinted in STRIKING STUFF by Jean A. Gittins, First published by 1 in 12 Publications Collective (1986) ISBN 0 948994 00 2 **p.91** An internet article, written in 2007 by someone called 'Steven'. https://libcom.org/library/notes-on-the-miners-strike-1984-1985; **p.92** Quote from David Douglas. *ASLEF Journal*, February 2014; **p.104** Quote from John Darwin, 1991; **pp.114–15** From *Sektion 20* by Paul Dowswell. Used by permission from Bloomsbury; **p.117** Leslie Collitt quote, © Guardian News & Media Ltd. 2015; **p.127** Quote from David Starkey, 2005, published in ''Gunpowder Plot was England's 9/11'' by Nick Britten. Used by Permission from *The Telegraph*.

Photo credits

p.2 © coward_lion – Fotolia; **p.3** *l* © Central Press/Getty Images *r* © stevanzz – Fotolia; **p.5** © Historic Environment Record, Cornwall Council; **p.8** *a* © Museum of London/Heritage Images/Getty Images, *b* © The Print Collector / Alamy, *c* © Jane Tyler, *d* © CSG CIC Glasgow Museums and Libraries Collections, *e* Image courtesy of www.keepcalm-o-matic.co.uk, *f* © Ullstein Bild / TopFoto; p.9 *g* © 2004 Topham Picturepoint/TopFoto, *i* © PA Photos / TopFoto, *j* © 2004 The Image Works / TopFoto; **p.11** © Zefrog / Alamy; **p.12** ©TopFoto; **p.13** © Lordprice Collection / Alamy; **p.14** © akg-images / Alamy; **p.17** © Glasshouse Images / Alamy; **p.20** © The Print Collector / Alamy; **p.21** © Lt. J W Brooke/IWM via Getty Images; **p.25** *t* © Alexander Meledin Collection / Mary Evans Picture Library, *b* © Mary Evans Picture Library; **p.26** *l* © World History Archive / Alamy, *r* © The Art Archive / Alamy; **p.27** © Paul Nash/ IWM via Getty Images; **p.28** © Willy Maley; **p.30** © ullsteinbild / TopFoto; **p.32** *t* © CSG CIC Glasgow Museums and Libraries Collections, *b* Courtesy Spanish Collection, Marx Memorial Library, London; **p.34** Photo © John D. Clare – Image courtesy of www.keepcalm-o-matic.co.uk; **p.38** Cartoon by Joseph Lee, Evening News, 19 November 1943 © Solo Syndication/Associated Newspapers Ltd. (photo: The British Cartoon Archive, University of Kent); **p.39** Cartoon by Illingworth, Daily Mail, 17 September 1944 © Solo Syndication/Associated Newspapers Ltd. Supplied by Llyfrgell Genedlaethol Cymru/The National Library of Wales; **p.40** Cartoon by Illingworth, Daily Mail, 17 September 1944 © Solo Syndication/Associated Newspapers Ltd. Supplied by Llyfrgell Genedlaethol Cymru/The National Library of Wales; **p.41** Cartoon by Illingworth, Daily Mail, 28 August 1944 © Solo Syndication/Associated Newspapers Ltd. Supplied by Llyfrgell Genedlaethol Cymru/The National Library of Wales; **p.42** Cartoon by Sidney 'George' Strube, Daily Express, 2 April 1945 © Northern & Shell Syndication and Licensing (photo: The British Cartoon Archive, University of Kent); **p.43** © Photos 12 / Alamy; **p.47** *t* © www.BibleLandPictures.com / Alamy, *b* Jews burnt at the stake, from the Nuremberg Chronicle by Hartmann Schedel (1440–1514), 1493 (colour woodcut), German School, (15th century) / © Bibliotheque Mazarine, Paris, France / Archives Charmet / Bridgeman Images; **p.48** © gekaskr – Fotolia; **p.49** © World History Archive / Alamy; **p.50** *t* © 2005 Roger-Viollet / Topfoto, *b* © Galerie Bilderwelt/Getty Images; **p.51** *t* © Weiner Library/ REX Shutterstock, *m* © Universal History Archive/Getty Images, *b* © Mary Evans Picture Library / Alamy; **p.52** *l* © Austrian Archives/ Corbis, *r* © Ullstein Bild / TopFoto; **p.53** Bundesarchiv, Bild 133-075 / Photographer: unknown; **p.54** *tr* © dpa/Corbis, *tl* © 2004 Topfoto, *br* © Sovfoto/UIG via Getty Images, *bl* © Everett Collection Historical / Alamy; **p.55** © ITAR-TASS Photo Agency / Alamy; **p.58** © Roger Viollet/Getty Images; **p.59** © Yad Vashem Archives 121GO2; **p.60** *t* © Pictorial Press Ltd / Alamy, *b* © Votava/Imagno/Getty Images; **p.61** © Mary Evans Picture Library / Alamy; **p.62** © Neil Bates; **pp.62–63** © The Keasbury-Gordon Photograph Archive / Alamy; **pp.64–65** © Popperfoto/Getty Images; **pp.66–67** © PA Photos / TopFoto; **pp.68–69** © PA Photos / TopFoto; **p.70** *t* © The March of the Women Collection / Mary Evans Picture Library, *b* © Museum of London/Heritage Images/Getty Images; **p.71** © Pictorial Press Ltd / Alamy; **p.72** © 2001 Topham Picturepoint/TopFoto; **p.73** © Museum of London/Heritage Images/Getty Images; **pp.74–75** © Pictorial Press Ltd / Alamy; **p.76** © Hulton-Deutsch/Hulton-Deutsch Collection/Corbis; **p.78** *t* © Jane Tyler, *b* © TopFoto; **p.79** © Jane Tyler; **p.80** © Jane Tyler; **p.84** © ZUMA Press, Inc. / Alamy; **p.85** *l* © Georges De Keerle/Getty Images, *r* © Sahm Doherty/The LIFE Images Collection/Getty Images; **pp.86–87** © PA Photos / TopFoto; **p.88** *t* © Neil Bates, *b* © Neil Bates; **p.89** © Neil Bates; **p.90** *l* © BRIAN HARRIS / Alamy, *r* © ANDREW YATES/AFP/Getty Images; **p.91** © Martin Jenkinson / Alamy; **p.92** © News Syndication; **p.94** © David Wright; **p.96** © 2004 Topham Picturepoint/TopFoto; **p.97** © Chronicle / Alamy; **p.98** © Pictorial Press Ltd / Alamy; **p.99** India: Japanese WWII propaganda poster depicting the miseries of life under the British Raj and the prosperity attainable through independence / © Pictures from History / Bridgeman Images; **pp.102–03** © Popperfoto/Getty Images; **p.109** *l* © ullsteinbild / TopFoto, *r* © INTERFOTO / Sammlung Rauch / Mary Evans Picture Library; **p.110** *l* © Eddie Gerald / Alamy, *tr* © ullsteinbild / TopFoto, *br* © ullsteinbild / TopFoto; **p.111** © laufer – Fotolia, *b* © stocktributor – Fotolia; **p.112** *l* © ullsteinbild / TopFoto, *r* © ullsteinbild / TopFoto; **pp.114–15** © Frank-Andree/iStock/Thinkstock; **p.116** © Steven May / Alamy; **p.117** © ullsteinbild / TopFoto; **p.120** © 2004 The Image Works / TopFoto; **p.121** © PA Photos / Topfoto; **p.124** *l* © World History Archive / Alamy, *r* © Intelligence & Terrorism Information Center Israel; **p.125** ©TopFoto; **p.126** © Jasmin Merdan – Fotolia; **p.133** © Loop Images Ltd / Alamy; **pp.134–35** Map data © 2015 Google; **p.137** © Kevin Allen / Alamy.

Contents

Investigating the twentieth century

Hiroshima

This series starts each book by studying an event which the author team thinks defines the age – the event which says most about what the period was like and best gives us a sense of the period. For this book, we have chosen the dropping of the atomic bomb on Hiroshima; pages 2–3 will give you a chance to consider what it tells us about the times.

The British scientist Ernest Rutherford had first 'split the atom' in 1917, although he thought that hopes that this might produce large amounts of energy were 'moonshine'.

He was wrong, of course, and during the Second World War the famous scientist Albert Einstein wrote to President Roosevelt of the USA warning him that the Nazis in Germany were trying to make an atomic bomb of immense destructive power. In 1942, the Manhattan Project – a research team assembled under US physicist Robert Oppenheimer – was set up and tasked to make an atomic bomb. On 16 July 1945 it successfully conducted a test explosion in the desert of Alamogordo, New Mexico.

At 8:15 a.m. on 6 August 1945, the American B29 bomber Enola Gay dropped the first atomic bomb (nicknamed 'Little Boy') on the Japanese town of Hiroshima. On 9 August the Americans dropped a second bomb ('Fat Man') on Nagasaki.

A

⬆ The Children's Peace Monument in Hiroshima.

B

A description of the human effects of the atomic bomb

> **TELEGRAM**
> --
> CONDITIONS APPALLING STOP CITY WIPED OUT EIGHTY PER CENT ALL HOSPITALS
> DESTROYED OR SERIOUSLY DAMAGED INSPECTED TWO EMERGENCY HOSPITALS
> CONDITIONS BEYOND DESCRIPTION STOP EFFECT OF BOMB MYSTERIOUSLY SERIOUS
> STOP MANY VICTIMS APPARENTLY RECOVERING SUDDENLY SUFFER FATAL RELAPSE
> DUE TO DECOMPOSITION WHITE BLOODCELLS ... NOW DYING IN GREAT NUMBERS

⬆ A telegram sent 30 August 1945 by Fritz Bilfinger of the International Red Cross.

In the shadow of Hiroshima…

The atomic bomb changed history forever.

The immediate effect was that the Japanese (who had been promising to fight to the death) surrendered, ending the Second World War. Later, the horrific effects of radiation poisoning became evident among the survivors.

In international politics, the bomb drove a permanent wedge of enmity between the USA and its **superpower** ally, the USSR (Russia). After 1949, when the USSR had also developed an atomic bomb, the world was thrown into a '**Cold War**', in which the two rival superpowers had enough nuclear weapons to destroy every living thing on earth many times over.

D

⬆ The Genbaku Dome of the Hiroshima Products Exhibition Hall (above) was just about the only building in Hiroshima to survive the blast, because it was directly underneath the explosion.

C

⬆ Until the USSR collapsed in 1991, humanity lived in fear of a 'nuclear armageddon', and there were many 'Ban the Bomb' marches in the 1950s and 1960s.

Activity

1 Discuss whether, and how, Hiroshima cast 'a shadow' on the world.
2 Working in a group of two or three, study the information on pages 2–3. Select what for you are the THREE most significant facts. For each, explain what it tells us about life in the twentieth century. Coming together as a class, compare the facts you selected and discuss: 'What does Hiroshima tell us about the twentieth century?'

The Hiroshima bomb exploded with the force of 20,000 tonnes of TNT.

- The mushroom cloud rose 15,000 metres into the air.
- The blast swept outwards at 500 miles per hour, flattening almost everything in a two-mile radius.
- The temperature in the centre of the explosion reached 300,000°C (fifty times hotter than the surface of the sun). People were vaporised, leaving nothing but their shadow.
- The Americans estimated that, of a population in Hiroshima of a quarter of a million, the bomb killed 66,000 and injured 69,000.
- 'Now, I am become Death, the destroyer of worlds', commented Robert Oppenheimer.
- 'We had adopted the moral standards of the barbarians in the dark ages,' complained US Chief of Staff Admiral Leahy.

Welcome to the twentieth century

Earlier in your course you studied a period usually called 'the Middle Ages', and then a period which many people term 'the Early Modern Era'. Later, you studied the years 1745–1901, a time which is often called the 'Industrial Revolution'. In this book, you are going to form an opinion about the twentieth century.

When, in 1930, the British historians W.C. Sellars and R.J. Yeatman wrote their comedy history *1066 And All That*, their final chapter – entitled 'A Bad Thing' – was very short. It said simply that, after the First World War:

> AMERICA *was thus clearly top nation, and History came to a .*

Of course, History did not come to a full stop in 1918, but it is true that Britain's dominance in the world did come to an end. In this respect Section 10 (about the end of the British Empire) sets the tone for the book. You will study certain events in Britain, but most of this book is about the world beyond Britain.

So what was the twentieth century like? In a century of two world wars, it is hard to disagree with the French writer Albert Camus, who called it 'an age of murder'.

Given the horrors of the Holocaust (see Section 5), and the anxieties of nuclear annihilation during the Cold War, some authors have gone even further, calling the period the 'century of genocide' and even 'the age of extinction'.

Much of the conflict during the century was caused by vicious political ideologies. For that reason, the socialist historian Eric Hobsbawm called the twentieth century 'the age of extremes'.

Activity

1 Where on the timeline would you mark:
 a) The Norman Conquest
 b) The execution of Charles I
 c) The Great Exhibition
 d) Hiroshima?
2 Comparing your life to that of the people in the nineteenth century, what is your initial feeling – was the twentieth century an age of progress?

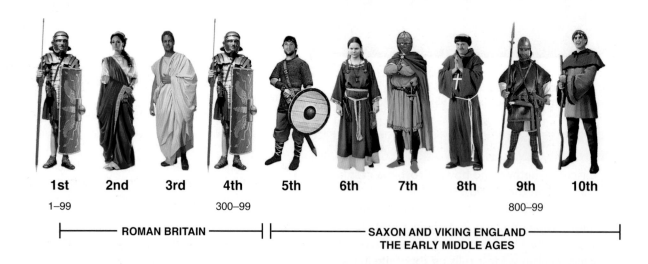

| 1st | 2nd | 3rd | 4th | 5th | 6th | 7th | 8th | 9th | 10th |

1–99   300–99   800–99

├── ROMAN BRITAIN ──┤ ├── SAXON AND VIKING ENGLAND ──┤
                        THE EARLY MIDDLE AGES

An Age of Progress?

But was *everything* bad? You have in your pocket a mobile phone with computing power as great as the computers which put a man on the moon, and access to knowledge more extensive than the largest Victorian library. So, when you study Section 6 on everyday life, you will see that the same technologies which murdered millions also led to improvements in living standards and human rights way beyond anything the world had ever seen. For this reason, the century has been called 'the age of information', but also 'the age of equality', 'the century of women' and even 'the century of leisure'.

In 2008, the American historian Walter G. Moss wrote *An Age of Progress?* He looked at the century's economic and technological miracles, and listed its disasters of war, politics and culture. His conclusion was that wisdom and morality had failed to keep pace with technological change. What is the point of a television, he asked, which could make truth and wisdom available to the masses … when all it does is offer whiter teeth and fresher breath?

As you study this book, you will want to keep the title of Moss's book – with its question mark – in mind. Was the twentieth century *An Age of Progress?*

Does the timeline show all of British history?

No! People have been living in Britain for many centuries.

This photograph shows ancient fields grouped around the site of a Celtic roundhouse (dating from about 400 BC) at Bosigran Farm in Cornwall. The present-day farm (top-left in photo) dates from the Middle Ages, but can you suggest where the Celtic roundhouse was situated (at the hub of the field system)?

Work out how far off the edge of page 4 this site would come on the timeline.

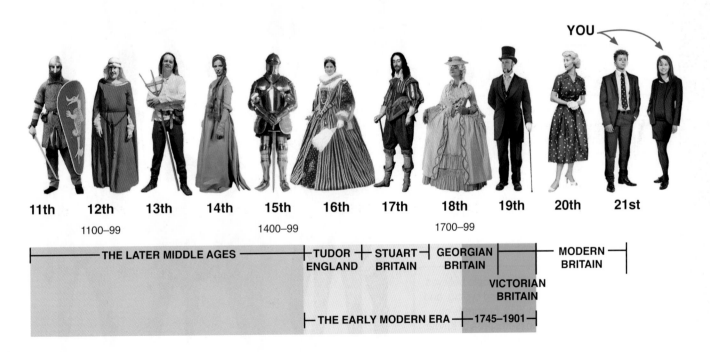

YOU

11th **12th** **13th** **14th** **15th** **16th** **17th** **18th** **19th** **20th** **21st**
1100–99 1400–99 1700–99

THE LATER MIDDLE AGES — TUDOR ENGLAND — STUART BRITAIN — GEORGIAN BRITAIN — MODERN BRITAIN

VICTORIAN BRITAIN

THE EARLY MODERN ERA — 1745–1901

Meet the people of the twentieth century

The people of the Middle Ages divided themselves into people who fought, prayed, and worked. The Early Modern Era ranked people by their status. The Victorians classed people as upper, middle or lower class.

Modern sociologists still identify social classes in British society, but group people into seven classes. These range from the 'elite' at the top (6 per cent of the population, with money, a cultured lifestyle and important friends) down to a deprived '**precariat**' at the bottom (15 per cent of the population). Other scholars, however, say that abstract ideas of 'class' are meaningless in our multicultural, internet world, and have identified the twentieth century as 'the age of individualism'.

The twentieth century saw the rise of social subgroups. Here are some of the more remarkable:

'Mods' wore suits and fur-collared anoraks, rode scooters, and danced to The Who. **'Rockers'** rode motorcycles, wore leathers, and preferred rock and roll. Both groups carried flick knives and bicycle chains as weapons. In 1964, gangs of Mods and Rockers horrified people when they fought pitched battles in holiday resorts on the south coast.

Skinheads were a violent British youth sub-culture dating from the 1960s. In the 1970s, they became increasingly known for their involvement in football hooliganism, the fascist 'National Front' movement, and racist attacks.

Flappers were young women who broke free of society's rules after the First World War. They abandoned long skirts and corsets in favour of short skirts and bobbed hair. They smoked, drank, used make-up, played sport, and danced the Charleston wildly in jazz clubs.

a) b) c)

The **Punks** were an anti-establishment culture which evolved in the late 1970s. They wore ripped jeans and jackets, safety pins and multiple piercings. Punk girls often went out in a black bin-liner. A punk trademark was their brightly-coloured, spiked 'Mohawk' hairstyle. They tried to shock – 'pogo-ing' wildly to aggressive rock music and throwing bags of urine at each other at concerts.

h) i) j)

Ramblers. In the 1930s, many people believed in healthy living, went walking and cycling, and stayed in YHA hostels. In 1932, hundreds of walkers took part in a mass-trespass at Kinder Scout, a mountain in the Peak District, and the Ramblers Association was formed in 1935.

Activity

1 From the descriptions, can you work out which people in the illustrations come from each sub-culture? Match the description to the letter above the illustrations.

2 Mark the different subcultures on a timeline; what do you notice?

3 Discuss as a class: how has the internet affected society?

'Teenagers' were invented in the 1950s – young people with money to spend and an attitude different from (and even hostile to) their parents. **Teddy Boys** wore 'drape suits' and 'drainpipe' trousers. They danced to Elvis Presley and rock and roll. Some formed violent gangs, and some took part in the Notting Hill race riots of 1958.

American psychologist Timothy Leary told the **Hippies** of the 1960s to 'Turn on, Tune in, Drop out'. They joined in communes, engaged in 'free love', and took drugs, notably cannabis and LSD. They attended pop festivals, and took part in Ban the Bomb marches and environmental protests.

The **Hells Angels** originated in America in 1948. On the surface, they were a motorcycle club. But they were anarchic, intimidating and violent – their logo was a death's head insignia from the Second World War. Membership was mainly white male, and they were accused of racism.

d)   e)   f)   g)

Goth subculture grew up in the 1980s. Goths dress in elaborate Victorian-style clothes, mainly in black and white, with black make-up and religious jewellery. They obsess about death and vampires, darkness, loneliness and depression.

k)   l)

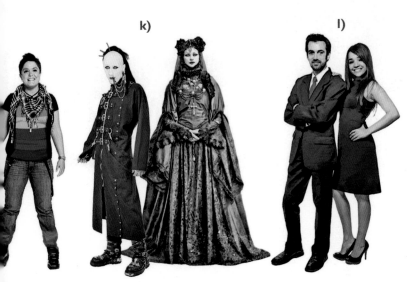

Yuppies. In the late 1980s and 1990s, while many young people were trapped in unemployment and poverty, 'young, upwardly-mobile professionals' gained well-paid jobs. They were 'cool Britannia' and openly flaunted their wealth – a stereotype mocked by comedian Harry Enfield's character 'Loadsamoney'.

Until 1967, homosexuality was a criminal offence, and gay people were derided and despised – even Home Secretary Lord Jenkins, who proposed the law to legalise homosexuality, called it a 'disability'. In 1972, the first **Gay Pride** rally was organised in London. Gradually, as attitudes modernised, gay people felt able to 'come out of the closet'.

7

A cataclysmic century

What do you know about the twentieth century?
Below are some of the headline events:

A The Suffragettes: In Britain 1903–14, the 'Suffragettes' used terrorist tactics to try to force Parliament to give women the vote.

C

Cable Street, Britain 1936: Jews, communists and anti-fascists fought a street battle to try to prevent a fascist march in the East End of London.

E Second World War 1939–45: A truly global conflict, in which perhaps 60 million people died. The consequences were immense, including the Holocaust, the division of Germany, the Cold War and Britain's Welfare State.

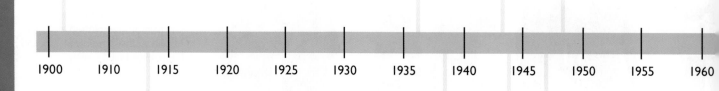

| 1900 | 1910 | 1915 | 1920 | 1925 | 1930 | 1935 | 1940 | 1945 | 1950 | 1955 | 1960 |

B First World War 1914–18: A truly global conflict, in which perhaps 37 million people died worldwide. The consequences were immense – the causes of the Russian Revolution, the rise of Hitler, and the Second World War have all been attributed to the First World War.

D

Spanish Civil War: In 1936–39, fascists and communists fought a **civil war** to see who would rule Spain – the fascists won.

F The Holocaust 1941–45: The Nazi attempt to exterminate the Jews.

G

The British Empire gradually gave independence to all but a few of its colonies after 1947.

I

The Miners' Strike Britain 1984–85: The miners fought – and lost – an industrial dispute with the government.

K

9/11: After the formation of **al-Qaeda** in 1990, extremist Islamic beliefs and terrorism spread all over the world. One act of terrorism was the 11 September 2001 attacks on the World Trade Center and the Pentagon in the USA.

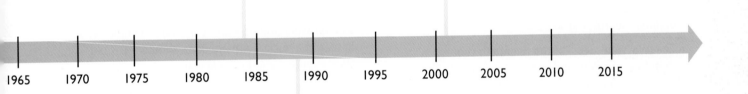

1965　1970　1975　1980　1985　1990　1995　2000　2005　2010　2015

H

The Welfare State: In 1944–48, the British government established a 'Welfare State' which included social security and unemployment benefits, council houses, free education and the National Health Service. The result was a significant improvement in everyday life – especially for the poor.

J

Berlin Wall: In 1989, the Berlin Wall came down in East Germany – the event which signified the end of the Cold War.

Activity

Working as a whole class:
1　Have you heard of any of the headline events on pages 8–9? (Don't worry if you have not.)
2　List together any other things you think you know about the twentieth century.

Studying the twentieth century

When historians study early history – for example, prehistoric times – the problem is, usually, lack of evidence. When you study the twentieth century, the problem is exactly the opposite! You are overwhelmed with facts and events, and the difficulty is knowing which facts to ignore.

When we came to write this textbook we knew that it would be impossible to tell you everything about everything – there aren't enough lessons in the twenty-first century! So we were forced to select – to choose for you a pathway through the data – so that you would end up with a broad knowledge about the century, but also with enough knowledge-in-depth to allow you to form a meaningful 'sense of period'.

The sections in this book, therefore, not only represent the dozen topics we regard as 'essential knowledge', they represent an overview of the different 'areas' of History – political, social and economic – across the century.

For the book itself, we have chosen to present the materials in three 'themes' (see the contents list at the start of the book).

An Age of Warfare

Most wars at the end of the nineteenth century were colonial wars. By the end of the century, there had been no major war for almost a century and, in 1864, the 'Geneva Convention' had been agreed, which defined the 'rules of war'.

The two 'total wars' of the twentieth century, therefore, shocked and changed the world. There was a war somewhere in the world every single year of the twentieth century, and some commentators have estimated that the number of deaths from war and internal conflicts was as high as 200 million.

The Post-War World

After 1945, Britain found itself struggling to survive as a major power in a world of industrial decline and high-tech globalisation. Meanwhile, the world was gripped by a 'Cold War' between the two superpowers (the USA and the USSR). People lived in fear of a nuclear armageddon should the 'Cold War' ever descend into real war.

The relief that people felt when the U SSR collapsed as a state in 1991, however, was short-lived, as they realised that a new threat – that of radicalised **jihadists** – had emerged.

Britain

In 1928, Britain finally became a full 'democracy' and, politically, the rest of the century became about how that democracy should work – and for whom.

For ordinary people in Britain, the century was one of medical miracles and increasing comfort – of a 'Welfare State', which after 1948 looked after its people 'from the cradle to the grave'. After the 1960s, the lives of people in Britain were revolutionised by developments in technology, and by social and cultural changes.

Activity

Look at events A–K on the timeline on pages 8–9. Which events would you place in each of the following categories:

▌ 'An Age of Warfare'
▌ 'Britain'
▌ 'The Post-War World'?

2

How would you have marked the 100th anniversary of the First World War?

How would you have marked the 100th anniversary of the First World War?

In early August 1914 two sides quickly formed and the First World War began: the Central Powers (Germany, Austria-Hungary and Italy, later to be joined by the Ottoman Empire) versus the Allies (Britain, France and Russia, later to be joined by the USA). Despite hopes that war would be over by Christmas, it would take four years and the deaths of 10 million people before the Allies finally claimed victory over the Central Powers on the eleventh minute of the eleventh hour of the eleventh month of 1918.

One hundred years later in November 2014, 888,246 ceramic poppies were 'planted' outside the Tower of London, one for each of the British and colonial soldiers who died in the First World War (1914–18). This section will focus on why this horrific war happened, what happened during the four years of fighting and its lasting impact. Your challenge at the end of this section, on page 27, will be to consider how you would have marked the 100th anniversary – do you think these poppies were a good idea?

A

⬆ The Tower of London poppy memorial, 2014. Do you think this was a fitting memorial?

Stepped Enquiry

Which historian's argument about the causes of the First World War do you agree with most?

The causes of the First World War are very complex. They have been argued over by historians in the century that has followed and will continue to be debated. On pages 11–19 we will look at three of these historians and your task is to decide which you agree with the most.

Enquiry Step 1: First evidence – asking questions

1 Read through the quotes on the right. Summarise each historian's argument into fewer than ten words.

2 In pairs think about any questions you might want to ask each historian.

Max Hastings:

> No one nation deserves all responsibility for the outbreak of war, but Germany seems to me to deserve most.

Gerhard Hirschfeld:

> The actual decision to go to war ... resulted from a fatal mixture of political misjudgement, fear of loss of prestige and stubborn commitments on all sides of a very complicated system of military and political **alliances** of European states.

Richard Evans:

> Serbia bore the greatest responsibility for the outbreak of WW1. Serbian **nationalism** and **expansionism** were profoundly disruptive forces and Serbian backing for the Black Hand terrorists was extraordinarily irresponsible.*

*See page 139

Was Max Hastings right to blame Germany for the First World War?

When assigning blame for an event in history, to say that one country or person deserves responsibility is a big statement. But Max Hastings firmly argues Germany was the main culprit, a view that was shared by the **Allies** after the war. The satirical cartoon below brilliantly summarises their argument.

> **Think**
>
> Look at Cartoon B. In what ways does the cartoonist try to influence you to believe that Germany was to blame?

B

HE WONT BE HAPPY TILL HE GETS IT

↑ A British cartoon of Kaiser Wilhelm II (leader of Germany) taking a bath.

Enquiry Step 2: Suggesting an answer

The cartoon above is very simplistic and one sided. As good historians we need to look at more evidence to try to prove or disprove an argument. This will help us begin to decide whether Max Hastings' argument is convincing.

1 Read the evidence on page 13. Copy the table and complete one row for each piece of evidence. An example has been done for you.

Evidence	How did this make war more likely?	To what extent was this Germany's fault?
Evidence 1: Triple Alliance	It meant more countries would be involved.	At most it was only a third Germany's fault as other countries were involved too.

2 When you have completed your table, discuss your results and decide:
   a) How far do you agree with Max Hastings' argument?
   b) Is this evidence sufficient to make a judgement?

Evidence 1: Triple Alliance

In 1882 Germany formed an alliance with Austria-Hungary and Italy. All three countries agreed to support each other if they were attacked. The Germans were worried about the French, who they had defeated in 1871, and wanted to protect themselves against retaliation.

Evidence 2: Kaiser Wilhelm II and Germany

Wilhelm II became ruler of Germany in 1888. Germany was a relatively new country, having only been formed in 1871 and Wilhelm was keen for it to show its power. He wanted to build Germany's empire, saying Germans wanted *'our place in the sun'*. He was prone to irrational outbursts and in an interview to the *Daily Telegraph* newspaper said *'You English are mad, mad, mad as March hares'*.

Evidence 3: Naval arms race

The British had the largest navy in the world at the end of the nineteenth century. The Germans realised that to get power they needed to compete, so began building up their own navy. In response to this the British designed a new ship, the Dreadnought, launched in 1906, which used the latest and greatest technology. Germany copied and built their own. By 1914 Britain had 29 and Germany had 17.

C

⬆ A Dreadnought battleship in 1907.

Evidence 4: Schlieffen Plan

In 1905 General Schlieffen, one of Germany's top military advisers, prepared a plan to attack France through Belgium in case a war began.

Evidence 5: First Moroccan Crisis

In 1905 Morocco was ruled by the French. However, some Moroccans were arguing for their independence. In March, Kaiser Wilhelm II landed in Morocco and rode a white horse into the capital Tangiers to support their cause. This deeply angered the French, but at a peace conference that followed they had to agree to lessen their control and make the Moroccan police independent.

Evidence 7: Blank cheque to Austria

In 1914, when trouble broke out in Sarajevo (read page 17), what should have been a local crisis that could have been dealt with by the Austro-Hungarians escalated as the Germans wrote a 'blank cheque', meaning they would help in any way they wished at whatever cost.

Evidence 6: Second Moroccan Crisis

In 1911 a rebellion broke out in Morocco. The French sent troops to crush it. The Germans reacted by sending the *Panther*, their biggest navy ship, to Morocco to protect German trade interests. The French were concerned that the Germans were trying to support the rebellion and take control. The British had to intervene to stop all-out war.

2

How would you have marked the 100th anniversary of the First World War?

Should we actually blame all of Europe for war in 1914?

So far you may agree with Max Hastings that Germany was mostly to blame for the war in 1914, but there is a lot of evidence that you have not yet seen. As you found out on page 11, Gerhard Hirschfeld, a German historian, says that the war happened because of *'stubborn commitments on all sides of a very complicated system'*. In this chapter we will develop our answer by looking at Hirschfeld's argument to see if we should actually blame *all* of Europe for the outbreak of war.

Enquiry Step 3a: Developing your answer

1 Below is a cartoon that appeared as a postcard in Germany in 1914. Locate the following countries and write down some words about what this German artist was suggesting about each country:
   - a) United Kingdom
   - b) France
   - c) Russia
   - d) Austria-Hungary
   - e) Germany
   - f) Ottoman Empire (modern-day Turkey)

2 Overall, what is the artist suggesting about Europe in 1914? Why might this lead to war?

D

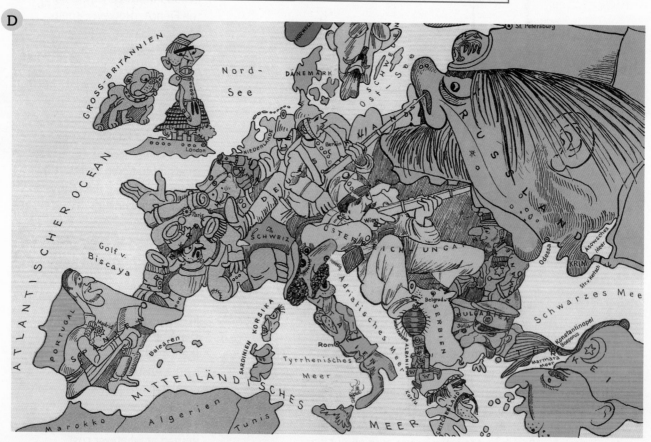

↑ A German postcard featuring a satirical map of Europe in 1914.

As the postcard above suggests, pre-war Europe was full of countries jostling for power. On page 15 you will find out about the six most powerful countries at the time. As you read the details, consider why they increased the likelihood of war.

RUSSIA

Size of army: 6 million
Number of battleships: 4
Population: 167 million
Size of empire: The largest single country in the world and the second biggest empire, but no overseas territories.
Desires: To expand its territory by taking areas from Austria-Hungary and the Ottomans. Encouraged Slavic independence in places like Serbia.

BRITAIN

Size of army: 1 million
Number of battleships: 29
Population: 46 million
Size of empire: The largest empire the world had ever seen with countries in North America, Asia and Africa.
Desires: To keep the 'balance of power' in Europe to prevent the emergence of threats to the British Empire.

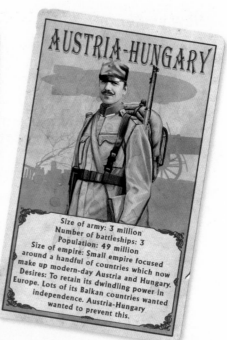

AUSTRIA-HUNGARY

Size of army: 3 million
Number of battleships: 3
Population: 49 million
Size of empire: Small empire focused around a handful of countries which now make up modern-day Austria and Hungary.
Desires: To retain its dwindling power in Europe. Lots of its Balkan countries wanted independence. Austria-Hungary wanted to prevent this.

GERMANY

Size of army: 4.5 million
Number of battleships: 17
Population: 65 million
Size of empire: Small but growing empire with countries in Africa and the Philippines.
Desires: To become the dominant power in Europe. It was jealous of Britain's wealth and wanted to catch up.

FRANCE

Size of army: 4 million
Number of battleships: 10
Population: 39 million
Size of empire: Medium-sized empire including large swathes of West Africa and parts of modern-day Vietnam.
Desires: As it had lost a war with Germany in 1871 it wanted to protect itself against another German attack.

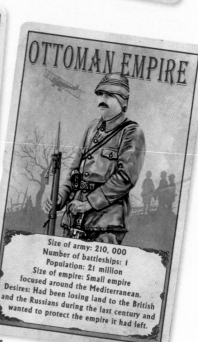

OTTOMAN EMPIRE

Size of army: 210, 000
Number of battleships: 1
Population: 21 million
Size of empire: Small empire focused around the Mediterranean.
Desires: Had been losing land to the British and the Russians during the last century and wanted to protect the empire it had left.

Enquiry Step 3b: Developing your answer

Read through the cards above.
1 Order the countries according to how powerful they were in 1914 (1 being the most powerful and 10 the least). Underneath, write a paragraph about why you have put them in this order.
2 Discuss with a partner how this situation might make war more likely. Share your answers with your class.

2

How would you have marked the 100th anniversary of the First World War?

New evidence

As you found out on page 13, the Germans, Austro-Hungarians and Italians formed an alliance in 1882. In retaliation the British, French and Russians* formed their own alliance, the Triple Entente, in 1907. Europe now had two very large, competing groups who would be prepared to support each other in a war.

* The Russians also agreed to support many other smaller 'Slav' countries in the Balkans, including Serbia. This would be crucial later on!

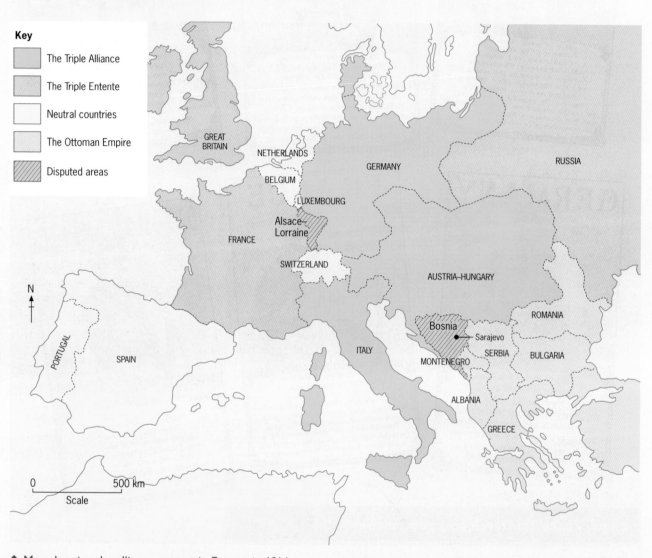

Key

- The Triple Alliance
- The Triple Entente
- Neutral countries
- The Ottoman Empire
- Disputed areas

⬆ Map showing the alliance system in Europe in 1914.

Enquiry Step 3c: Developing your answer

1 Consider the following question. Did the alliance system make war MORE or LESS likely? Write down your answer.

2 Who do you most agree with now about why the war began – Max Hastings or Gerhard Hirschfeld?

Did the Serbians start the First World War or merely make it happen sooner?

As you read on pages 14–16 there was a lot of tension in Europe in 1914. The fuse of this bomb was lit by the Serbians on 28 June 1914. Richard J. Evans, one of the most prominent historians in the UK, believes that their actions 'bore the greatest responsibility for the outbreak of WW1'.

As a class, read the story below of 28 June 1914 and see if you can work out why this was the trigger for four years of war.

This is the tale of a group of incompetent assassins who managed to start a war. But before we get to them we need to start much further back in the nineteenth century. In 1876, Serbia, a small country in the Balkans, had managed to gain independence from the Ottoman Empire, but many Serbians in neighbouring Bosnia remained under the control of another empire, led by the Austro-Hungarians. The Serbian government would not tolerate this. A secret plan was hatched.

The Serbian government formed a terrorist group, the Black Hand, led by Dragutin Dimitrijević who had the nickname of 'the Bee'. The Bee decided that to win Bosnian independence the Black Hand would assassinate a prominent member of the royal family of Austria-Hungary. The Bee put together his best men for the job – we will see whether you agree with that in the minute!

In June 1914 the opportunity arose. Archduke Franz Ferdinand, the heir to the throne, was visiting Sarajevo, the capital of Bosnia, to inspect troops, despite being warned by Austrian spies and even by Pasic, the Prime Minister of Serbia, that there could be trouble.

On the planned day the assassination team assembled along the River Miljacka, each ready to kill the Archduke as his car passed them. Six men, six chances. The Archduke left the barracks and the men were ready, except not that ready... The first two, Mehmedbašić and Čubrilović, failed to act, watching as the car went past! The car approached the next assassin, Čabrinović. He threw his bomb...but the timing on the detonator was wrong and it bounced off the car, only to explode once they had driven away. Čabrinović, not waiting to see if he had been successful,

quickly took measures to evade capture. He swallowed his poisonous cyanide pill and to be doubly sure jumped into the river to drown himself. Unfortunately, the pill was too old and the river was only 13 cm deep so his suicide failed and he was quickly apprehended by the police.

After stopping to see what had happened, the car driver quickly sped away. The next three assassins, Popović, Princip and Grabež, should have acted now... but in the panic they also failed to act. The Bee's team had failed.

BUT... this is not the end of the tale. After his meeting at the Town Hall, Franz Ferdinand and his wife Sophie returned to their car. The assassins meanwhile were downbeat and had given up. Gavrilo Princip, leaving the others, made his way to Schillers delicatessen for a spot of lunch. On leaving the delicatessen Princip looked up in surprise. By total coincidence Franz Ferdinand's car was right in front of him! With almost no time to think Princip pulled out his pistol and shot two bullets. One pierced through the Archduke's neck, the second hit his wife's stomach. Both would die later that day. Princip was immediately arrested. The first step had been taken; the chain reaction that led to war had begun.

This photo shows the moment after the assassination as Gavrilo Princip was arrested by the police.

2

How would you have marked the 100th anniversary of the First World War?

The assassination of Franz Ferdinand was like someone lighting the fuse of a bomb. In this case the fuse would last 37 days and at its end would be a war that lasted four years. In the diagram below, read what happened in what people now called the July Crisis, before discussing whether you agree that Richard Evans' theory – the Serbians bore the most responsibility – was correct.

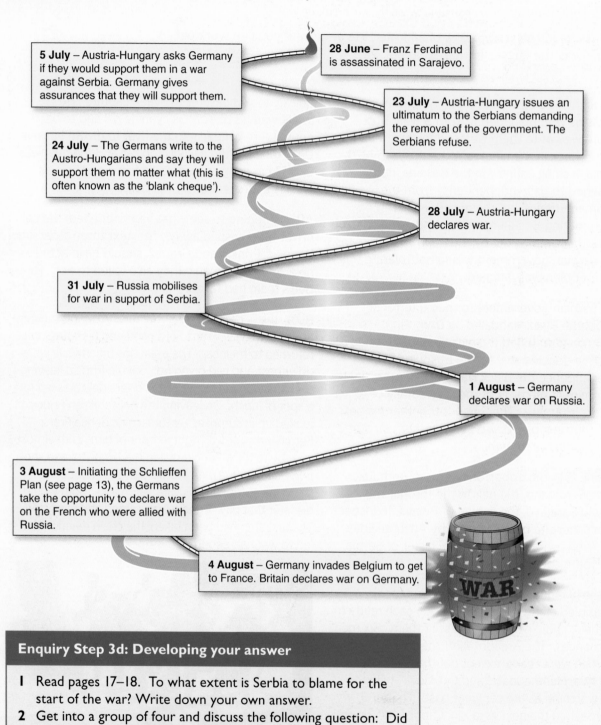

5 July – Austria-Hungary asks Germany if they would support them in a war against Serbia. Germany gives assurances that they will support them.

28 June – Franz Ferdinand is assassinated in Sarajevo.

23 July – Austria-Hungary issues an ultimatum to the Serbians demanding the removal of the government. The Serbians refuse.

24 July – The Germans write to the Austro-Hungarians and say they will support them no matter what (this is often known as the 'blank cheque').

28 July – Austria-Hungary declares war.

31 July – Russia mobilises for war in support of Serbia.

1 August – Germany declares war on Russia.

3 August – Initiating the Schlieffen Plan (see page 13), the Germans take the opportunity to declare war on the French who were allied with Russia.

4 August – Germany invades Belgium to get to France. Britain declares war on Germany.

Enquiry Step 3d: Developing your answer

1 Read pages 17–18. To what extent is Serbia to blame for the start of the war? Write down your own answer.

2 Get into a group of four and discuss the following question: Did the Serbians start the war or just make it happen sooner?

3 As a class discuss what you think of Evans' argument (see page 11). Do you agree with him more than Hastings or Hirschfeld?

Enquiry Step 4: Concluding your enquiry

By now you should have developed a pretty good idea about which of the three historians you think is most convincing about the cause of the war. The instructions below will help you consolidate your opinion and then write a final conclusion to the stepped enquiry question:

Which historian's argument about the causes of the First World War do you agree with most?

1 This is a causation question. You should be able to say why each of the following contributed to the start of the First World War. Discuss each with a partner.

The assassination of Franz Ferdinand	The personality of Kaiser Wilhelm	The Triple Entente
The Triple Alliance	The Schlieffen Plan	The naval arms race	Serbian nationalists
July Crisis	Imperialism (the existence of large competing empires)	Moroccan Crises

BUT looking at these causes in isolation is a bit basic. Great historians will consider:
▌ how causes are linked
▌ how each cause helps build towards an event.

To help you to do this, complete Activities 2 and 3.

2 Write the causes (above, in blue) randomly over a double page in your book. Leave space between them. Add the following codes to the causes. Include a key to these codes on your page too.
▌ LT = long-term causes – those that stretch back to earlier than 1900.
▌ ST = short-term causes – those that happened between 1900 and 1913.
▌ C = catalysts – those events that happened in 1914.

3 Now consider which causes are linked. Draw lines between those that are linked and along them write a brief explanation. We have included an example below.

Assassination of Franz Ferdinand ——————————————————————— The Triple Alliance

The death of Franz Ferdinand triggered the alliance system following Austria-Hungary's attack

You might find all the connections on your page look messy, but that is okay: messy means lots of thinking.

4 Now you should be ready to write an answer to the enquiry question:

Which historian's argument about the causes of the First World War do you agree with most?

Justify your answer and try to bring in some of the sophisticated analysis that you did in Activities 2 and 3.

5 We started this section with the poppies memorial (page 11) and later you will design your own. The poppies only focus on Britain. Is this right? Would you do it differently? How might you include what you think about the cause of the war into your memorial? Jot down any ideas you have.

2

How would you have marked the 100th anniversary of the First World War?

Was it all just 'mud, rats and poppies' in the First World War?

On pages 11–19 we looked at the causes of the war; now we will look at what happened in the war. If you asked people for a defining image of the First World War they would probably say one or all of the following – mud, rats and poppies. However, this is a very British view of the war from the Western Front. On pages 20–23 we compare the experience at the Western Front to the other theatres of war to examine whether 'mud, rats and poppies' was true no matter where you were fighting.

The Western Front

One of the largest theatres of war was the Western Front, a line stretching from Switzerland to the North Sea in Belgium.

In 1914, the Germans were initially very successful, but by September the British and the French had halted their advance. Both sides dug in along meandering **trenches**. Despite some major offensives from both sides this line of trenches barely moved in four years. Some very famous battles on the Western Front ended in vast numbers of deaths, like the Somme described on page 21. After the war poppies grew over these fields and many people said their red colour represented the blood that had been spilt there.

In an effort to break the stalemate new technology was developed, including flame throwers, poison gas, aircraft and tanks. Much of this caused devastating harm to those fighting on the front lines.

In late 1918 the Allies gained the upper hand and advanced, leading to a German surrender that brought the end of war to all the theatres.

A

⬆ British soldiers advancing under cover of gas and smoke, France. A break in the German lines is made during the Battle of the Somme. Photo taken by a captured prisoner.

Which were the main countries involved?

Entente Powers: UK, France, Belgium, USA

Central Powers: Germany, Austria-Hungary

Killed, wounded, captured or missing:

Entente Powers: 7.9 million

Central Powers: 5.6 million

B

← The Mark I tank surrounded by some of the British infantry from 122nd Brigade, 15 September 1916.

Activity

What evidence can you find on pages 20–21 to prove that rats, mud and poppies are the defining features of the Western Front in the First World War?

C

Harry Patch's testimony of life on the Western Front. Patch was the last surviving 'Tommy' but died in 2009.

From … June 1917 – until I left … December 1917, … I never had a bath. I never had any clean clothes. And … on the way home they took every stitch of clothing off us: vest, shirt, pants, everything and they burnt it all. It was the only way to get rid of the lice.

The trenches were about six feet deep, about three feet wide – mud, water, a **duckboard** if you were lucky. You slept on the firing step, if you could, shells bursting all around you. Filthy.

Rats as big as cats. Anything they could gnaw, they would – to live. If you didn't watch it, they'd gnaw your shoe laces. … As you went to sleep, you would cover your face with a blanket and you could hear the damn things run over you.

If any man tells you he went into the front line and he wasn't scared – he's a liar. You were scared from the moment you got there.

CASE STUDY: The Battle of the Somme

The Battle of the Somme was intended to be the big breakthrough in the war. For the week before 1 July 1916 the Allies pounded German lines with over 1.6 million shells with the aim of destroying their trenches before sending in soldiers. However, the German trenches were very heavily fortified and the shells did not do the damage the Allies had hoped for. On the morning of 1 July the British officers were so confident that the shells had worked that they told the soldiers to walk over no-man's-land, the area between the British and German trenches, to the German side. As soon as they heard the starting whistle the Germans climbed out of hiding and took position. The 11 British divisions were walking towards their slaughter as the German machine guns began. On that morning alone there were 60,000 casualties, of whom 20,000 were dead.

The battle continued for two weeks before reaching a stalemate from July to September. In September General Haig renewed the offensive using a brand new technology, tanks, shown in picture B above. In October, rain turned the battlefield into a quagmire. By the middle of November when the battle ended the British had gained only 8 km of land at the cost of over 1 million wounded or dead, making it one of the bloodiest battles in history.

The First World War – the first global war

The First World War was truly a global war and was fought not just in the trenches of the Western Front. Pages 22–23 introduce you to the other 'theatres' of war and should help you to think more about whether this was just 'mud, rats and poppies'.

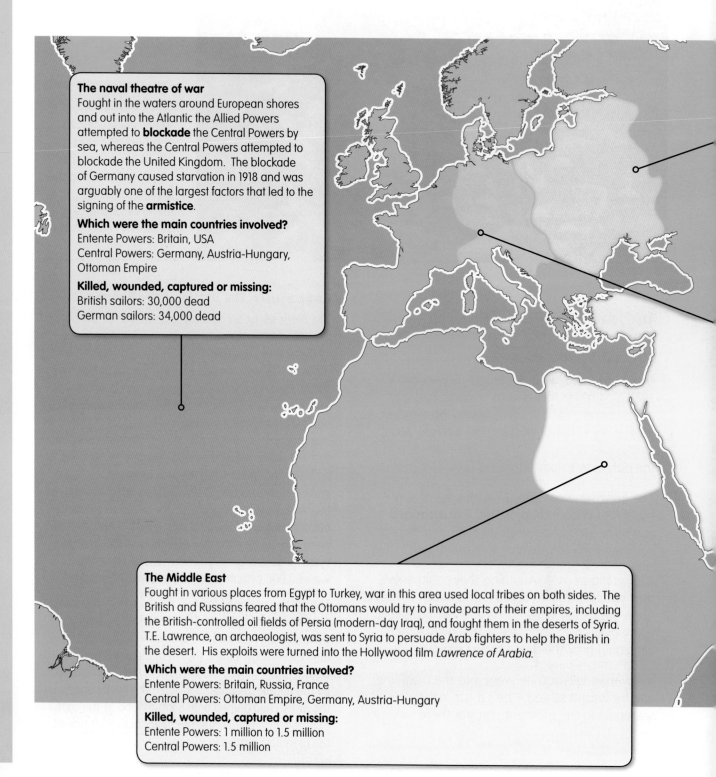

The naval theatre of war
Fought in the waters around European shores and out into the Atlantic the Allied Powers attempted to **blockade** the Central Powers by sea, whereas the Central Powers attempted to blockade the United Kingdom. The blockade of Germany caused starvation in 1918 and was arguably one of the largest factors that led to the signing of the **armistice**.

Which were the main countries involved?
Entente Powers: Britain, USA
Central Powers: Germany, Austria-Hungary, Ottoman Empire

Killed, wounded, captured or missing:
British sailors: 30,000 dead
German sailors: 34,000 dead

The Middle East
Fought in various places from Egypt to Turkey, war in this area used local tribes on both sides. The British and Russians feared that the Ottomans would try to invade parts of their empires, including the British-controlled oil fields of Persia (modern-day Iraq), and fought them in the deserts of Syria. T.E. Lawrence, an archaeologist, was sent to Syria to persuade Arab fighters to help the British in the desert. His exploits were turned into the Hollywood film *Lawrence of Arabia*.

Which were the main countries involved?
Entente Powers: Britain, Russia, France
Central Powers: Ottoman Empire, Germany, Austria-Hungary

Killed, wounded, captured or missing:
Entente Powers: 1 million to 1.5 million
Central Powers: 1.5 million

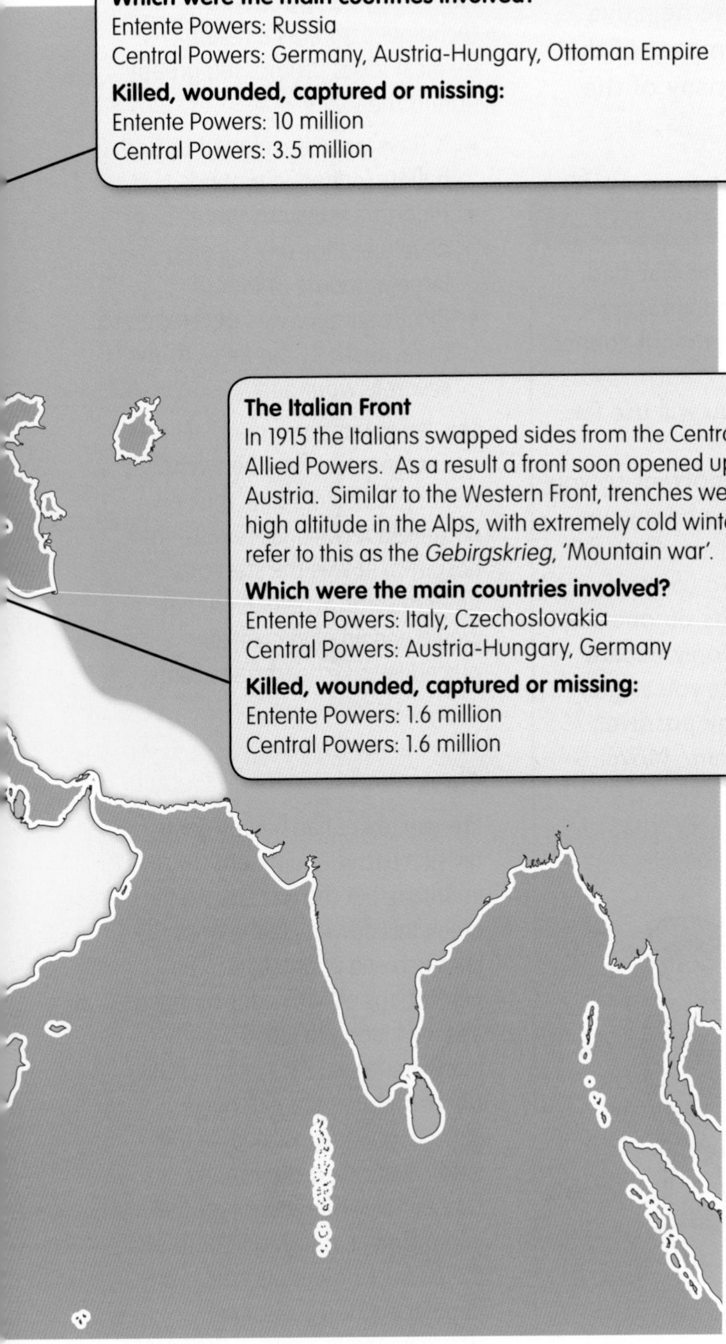

The Eastern Front

Fought along a line stretching from the Baltic Sea in the north to the Black Sea in the south, a distance of nearly 1,000 miles! This long distance meant that the battle lines were far more fluid and often trenches were not dug, but the clashes here were as bloody as the Western Front. Russian failures led to great anger amongst its people and arguably led to the downfall of their monarch, the Tsar.

Which were the main countries involved?

Entente Powers: Russia
Central Powers: Germany, Austria-Hungary, Ottoman Empire

Killed, wounded, captured or missing:

Entente Powers: 10 million
Central Powers: 3.5 million

The Italian Front

In 1915 the Italians swapped sides from the Central Powers to the Allied Powers. As a result a front soon opened up between Italy and Austria. Similar to the Western Front, trenches were dug in, but at high altitude in the Alps, with extremely cold winters. The Germans refer to this as the *Gebirgskrieg*, 'Mountain war'.

Which were the main countries involved?

Entente Powers: Italy, Czechoslovakia
Central Powers: Austria-Hungary, Germany

Killed, wounded, captured or missing:

Entente Powers: 1.6 million
Central Powers: 1.6 million

Activity

1 Write down three words to summarise each theatre of war on pages 22–23.
2 Why is a dominant image of the First World War 'muds, rats and poppies', when these weren't features of the fighting beyond the Western Front? Suggest a reason for this.
3 The poppies memorial (see page 11) uses a symbol from the Western Front (poppies grew over the trenches after the war). Is the memorial representative of the whole war? Do you think it needs to be? Jot down any further ideas you have to design your own memorial later.

The Big Picture

2 How would you have marked the 100th anniversary of the First World War?

Does the negative impact of the First World War outweigh the positive impact?

The obvious impact of the First World War was death and destruction on a large scale, but this was certainly not the only impact. In fact, the First World War had both positive and negative results. On pages 24–7 you will be asked to weigh up the evidence and decide whether the positive or the negative impacts were strongest. This is important as the impact of the war sets the scene for the twentieth century and many of the themes in the rest of this book begin here.

Activity

As a class split into two groups – one will argue that the war had a positive impact, the other will argue that the war had a negative impact. You are all going to debate this topic in an argument tunnel! Before you do this you all need to prepare…

1 Read pages 24–7 and make a list of the evidence you will use for your half of the debate.
2 Rank your evidence from very important to not important so you know which pieces of evidence are best for trying to beat your opponents.

Now you are ready for your argument tunnel. Set two rows of chairs facing each other. The positive impact group sits on one side, the negative impact group sits on the other. You can only debate with the person directly opposite you. Make sure that you argue which impacts are most important. After 1 minute the positive impacts side should all move up one chair. Debate again. Move. Repeat. Do this ten times!

Extra hard challenge: On the last turn swap sides of the argument and argue the opposite!

Medicine

To cope with the large number of wounded soldiers, doctors experimented with new techniques and, as a result, medical ideas progressed greatly during the war.

- X-Rays were developed to find bullets lodged in wounds.
- Blood transfusions were developed for those losing large amounts of blood.
- Plastic surgery was developed to reconstruct the faces of the severely wounded.

This led to improved medical ideas and surgery for all in the twentieth century as doctors took the new battlefield techniques back to their hospitals. It was the start of a modern surgical revolution that would end up with complex procedures like heart transplants.

Class

Pre-war, there had been a great division between different classes in Britain, but the war started to break this down. On the front lines rich and poor mixed. The perceptions of both sides changed as they fought and died together in the trenches. As a result of this, the **franchise** was extended, giving working-class people the vote. Political parties like the Labour Party that fought for the improvement of the conditions of the poorest classes became more popular and the government slowly began to improve the lives of the working class with 'homes fit for heroes'.

Russian Revolution, 1917

Tsar Nicholas II, the Russian monarch, was not a great leader and the war highlighted his inadequacies. By 1917 the people of Russia were starving and fighting a losing battle on the Eastern Front. They could not tolerate it any longer, it was time for revolution! In February 1917, protests on the streets of Petrograd grew so large that Nicholas II was forced to **abdicate**. The government that followed was not much better and despite the public asking for an end to the war they bitterly continued the fight. This brought the people to revolution a second time. In October the **Bolsheviks**, led by Lenin, established a communist government, that would rule until 1991. From Russia, communism spread to other countries, like East Germany (see pages 106–119), and communist ideology played a part in other wars, such as the Spanish Civil War, where the Soviets funded the Republican army (see pages 28–33).

⬆ Soldiers and workers on the streets of Petrograd during the October Revolution, 1917.

⬆ A group of young women partying in the 1920s. These 'flappers' had brave new fashions, ideas and independence.

The changing role of women

Pre-war, the Suffragettes, a women's organisation fighting for the right to vote, had failed to convince the government to make a change. However, with men off fighting the war, women had to take over their jobs. In particular, carrying out the hard and dangerous work in the munitions factories that were supplying the front lines. As an acknowledgement of their contribution the government passed the Representation of the People Act in 1918 giving women over 30 the vote, followed in 1928 by the Equal Franchise Act which gave them the same voting rights as men. Women's self-perception also changed – gaining confidence and independence through their role in the war led to the more outgoing styles and behaviour in the 1920s.

The Big Picture

2

How would you have marked the 100th anniversary of the First World War?

Nationalism

⬆ Adolf Hitler, German politician and the leader of the Nazi Party, at a rally, 1923.

Patriotism was high before the war but it was inflated by the conflict and even higher after. Nationalism, the feeling of strong identification with your nation and extreme patriotism, grew all over the continent. This was particularly pronounced in Germany, where people felt they had been humiliated by the war. Some blamed minority groups for losing the war, such as Jewish people, and extreme anti-Semitic nationalist groups formed and gained support, including the Nazi Party. When the Nazis came to power in 1933 they began a series of anti-Semitic policies, which would escalate to the Holocaust during the Second World War (see pages 46–61).

Death and psychological impact

The First World War led to the death of between 8 and 10 million people in total, but some countries suffered more than others. The Germans and Russians each lost around 2 million people. The number of wounded was even larger, with estimates of between 22 and 24 million people. Many were deeply psychologically scarred by what they had seen during the war. The term 'shell shock' was coined to describe the trauma suffered by some soldiers as a result of battle on the front lines. Britain, in particular, had relied on soldiers from her Empire to make up the army, for example over 1 million Indian men volunteered. Many of these men also died and suffered psychological trauma and as a result their countrymen wanted something in return. In many parts of the British Empire calls for greater self-governance began and British control began to unravel (see pages 94–105).

⬆ British soldiers with wounded German soldiers at La Boisselle, the Somme, France 1918.

Culture

Moved by what they saw on the front lines, a handful of men produced poetry, art and music to reflect their war experience. The poetry of Wilfred Owen, the art of Paul Nash and the music of Ivor Gurney contributed to the culture of Britain. These artworks continue to be studied and heralded as pieces that define the age.

⬆ *The Menin Road*, circa 1919, by Paul Nash, depicts the desolation of the front line.

The Treaty of Versailles

In 1919, the Allies met at the Palace of Versailles to discuss what punishments Germany should face. The three most significant Allies (Britain, France and the USA) led proceedings. Very harsh penalties were set, including a repair bill of £6.6 billion, a reduction of the German army to a tiny 100,000 men with no air force or submarines, and finally a significant amount of German territory was lost to France and Poland. The German people were furious with their politicians for agreeing to the Treaty, and this formed the backdrop to the Nazi rise to power in the 1930s. As a result, some historians argue that the Treaty is where the long-term causes of the Second World War began.

Think

If a German student was completing the activity on page 24, would they view the evidence and rank its importance in the same way?

Activity

We started this section on page 11 by asking how you would have marked the 100th anniversary of the First World War and whether the poppies outside the Tower of London were a fitting memorial. The poppies, a symbol of the Western Front, represent the death and destruction of the war, but as you have just debated there is a lot more to the war.

1 Look back at the ideas about your memorial you collected on pages 19 and 23. Do they encapsulate everything you want to remember about the war?

2 Also consider the following question: What is the function of a memorial? Should you incorporate the positive impact of the war into your design? Discuss this in pairs.

3 Now you should be ready to produce your final design incorporating everything you have learnt about the causes, the war itself and its impact. Draw your memorial in the middle of a blank piece of paper and add annotations around it to justify your design.

Why did James Maley go to Spain in 1936?

In April 2007, during the cup-tie between Celtic and St Johnstone at Hampden Park football ground in Glasgow, two 30ft-long banners were unfurled. Quoting the Spanish slogan used by the defenders of Madrid during the Spanish Civil War, 'They shall not pass,' the banners said: 'James Maley R.I.P.' and 'No pasarán'.

Why would Scottish football fans in 2007 wave banners that link back to events in Spain in the 1930s? The answer to this questions lies with the gentleman named on the banners, James Maley. He was a native of Glasgow and a life-long Celtic fan, who passed away on 9 April 2007. You can see a photograph of James in Picture A.

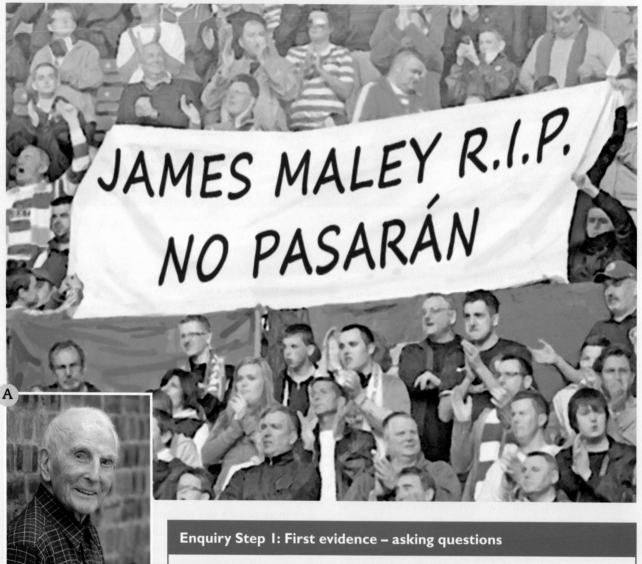

A

↑ A recent photo of James Maley prior to his death in 2007.

Enquiry Step 1: First evidence – asking questions

1 Why might James Maley have gone to Spain in 1936?

2 What reasons can you think of as to why anyone might want to get involved in a war? You might like to think back to why soldiers decided to fight in the First World War. Make a list of reasons in your book.

This enquiry is about why James Maley went to Spain in 1936. By carrying out the enquiry you will find out what was happening in Spain in 1936 and how this was, in many ways, a forerunner of the bigger events of the Second World War. You will also develop an understanding of why people in Glasgow in the early twenty-first century might still be proud of what James did in 1936.

James' story was commemorated in the song 'These Hands' by a band from Glasgow called The Wakes.

'These Hands'

I take a look at you old man,
as you sit in your chair
You can be almost anyone
For all I know or I care
But on your chest is a red star
From the days long gone by
of a proud fighting past
For a cause you held high
Son we set out from Glasgow
To the war torn Spain
Brave socialist fighters
from a Scottish Brigade
Not knowing our fate
or what would befall
But for justice and freedom
were prepared to give all
(Chorus)
And these hands fought the Fascists
at Jarama in Spain
My heart beats for justice
until my dying day
I never set out for glory
but I'd my part to play
In the fight against Franco
at Jarama in Spain

For five long weeks we waited
to be handed a gun
They drove us into the fighting
under Spain's blazing sun
And the fires of hell don't compare
to the battle that day
In the heat of Jarama
Seven thousand were slain
But we ran out of bullets
taken by Franco's men
To Talavera de la Reina
and then moved on again
The Calton had never
seemed so far away
as I lay in that prison in Salamanca
in Spain
(Chorus)
So take a look at me now son
and the star on my chest
Some of us gave up everything
For the cause of the left
The deeds that we've done
and the part that we played
in the fight against Franco
at Jarama in Spain

Enquiry Step 2: Suggesting an answer

Read the lyrics of the song 'These Hands'. What can you work out about James' adventures?

1 Make a list of anything that you can say about James with some degree of certainty.

2 What questions do you have? Are there any words you do not understand?

3 At this stage what do you think the connection is between James and events in Spain? Suggest your own hypothesis in answer to the question: Why did James Maley go to Spain in 1936?

In your hypothesis from Enquiry Step 2 on page 29, you probably worked out that James Maley went to Spain to fight for a cause. Now it is time to dig deeper and find out a bit more about what motivated him.

If we are to make sense of the events in which James was caught up, we need to find out more about European politics in the 1930s and about what was happening in Spain. The fact files below give an overview of the main political systems in Europe in the 1930s, and the map on page 31 shows the events in Spain.

Fact File: The USSR and communism

In the 1930s the USSR (also known as the Soviet Union) was a communist country. This had been the case since the Russian Revolution of 1917. The Soviet Union of the 1930s was ruled by Josef Stalin, who was effectively a dictator. All other political parties were banned and citizens had few rights – their lives were tightly controlled by the government. The police had powers to arrest and detain anyone suspected of 'crimes against the state'. These people were often murdered or sent to live in prison camps known as Gulags. All property, businesses and industry in the USSR were owned and controlled by the state. Theoretically everyone was equal, although Communist Party bosses enjoyed a more privileged lifestyle.

Fact File: Spain and socialism

The Spanish Popular Front came to power in February 1936 under the leadership of Manuel Azaña. This new socialist government believed that social reform could be achieved through parliamentary means, as opposed to being instigated by violent revolution. So, while the ends were similar to those of the communists, the means were more peaceful and democratic. Efforts were made to extend rights to women, to begin land reforms in favour of the Spanish agricultural workers and to reduce the size of the army.

Fact File: Nazi Germany and fascism

Since January 1933 Germany had been controlled by the fascist National Socialist German Workers' Party (Nazis) under the leadership of Adolf Hitler. Following the passing of the Enabling Act in March 1933, Hitler was dictator of Germany. All political parties were banned and their leaders often had to go into hiding or exile to escape prison or murder. German people were free to own property but major industries such as armaments were controlled by the state.

Fact File: Fascist Italy

Since 1922 Italy had been a fascist country under the rule of Benito Mussolini.

In fascist countries, the leader was in overall control. There were no elections and all other political parties were banned. Just as in Nazi Germany citizens had few rights, with their lives tightly controlled by the party. The Italian police had the power to arrest and detain anyone suspected of 'crimes against the state'. People in fascist Italy could own their own property and businesses were sometimes privately owned.

Fact File: The United Kingdom and democracy

Democratic countries such as Britain allowed their citizens the right to choose their government every four or five years, with different political parties to choose from. While Britain had a monarchy, its powers were weak and laws were made in Parliament. Citizens had basic rights such as free speech and freedom of the press, as well as the right to a fair trial. The police were accountable to the government and people, meaning that their powers were limited. British people could own their own property and businesses were often privately owned.

Enquiry Step 3a: Developing your answer

1 Look at the fact files on page 30.
   a) Summarise the main beliefs in a sentence or two.
   b) If James Maley had grown up with a strong belief in democratic government, what do you think his attitude would have been towards Nazi Germany and Fascist Italy?
2 Look at the map below.
   a) What actions were taken by the fascists in Spain?
   b) What actions were taken by Italy and Germany?
   c) What might James Maley have travelled to Spain to protect?
3 Revisit your hypothesis from Enquiry Step 2. Do you want to make any changes to it?

1936 The Socialist Popular Front won elections in Spain. Led by Manuel Azana, the Spanish Republic quickly introduced reforms such as giving women the vote, giving land to the poor peasant farmers and reducing the size of and spending on the army.

17 July 1936 Having been banished to Spanish Morocco by the new government, army leaders under the command of General Fransisco Franco launched a *coup* to overthrow the government. Spain was at **civil war**. On the one side there was a right-wing coalition of fascists and **monarchists** with army backing, known as the Nationalists. On the other side were the supporters of the new Socialist Republic.

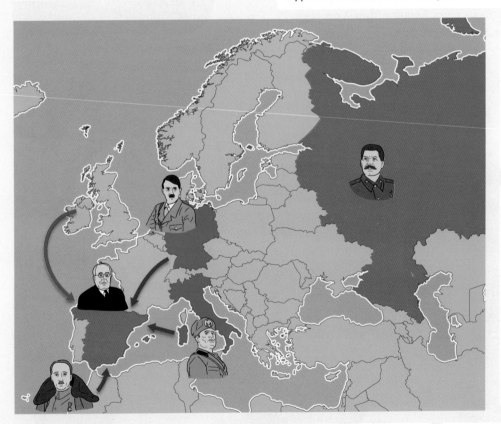

From late July 1936, Franco began to receive military aid from Germany and fascist Italy. Hitler, for instance, sent planes and pilots to help transport the Spanish right-wing military forces, garrisoned in Morocco, across to Spain.

From October 1936, the forces of the Republic began to receive aid from Communist Russia. At the same time volunteers from around the world began to head for Spain to fight to protect the socialist government. These volunteers eventually formed what became known as the International Brigades. One of these volunteers was James Maley.

1939: Madrid fell to the Nationalists. The Spanish Civil War was over. Spain then had a government modelled on General Franco's own version of autocratic fascism. Spain would remain a fascist country until Franco's death in 1975.

1938: the Republicans lost more key battles such as the Battle of Ebro. The International Brigades left Spain.

Summer 1937: Republicans lost control of the important city of Bilbao.

1937: Nationalists started a major offensive against the capital, Madrid. The International Brigades played an important part in resisting this offensive. Despite a successful defence of Madrid, later in the year the Republicans suffered heavy losses in the bombing of the city of Guernica.

Stepped Enquiry

We now need to know a little more about James Maley's life in order to cement our understanding of why he decided to go and fight in Spain.

Enquiry Step 3b: Developing your answer further

1 Read the story of James Maley's life on page 33. Make a list of things that might have persuaded James to fight in Spain. You could organise these ideas according to the headings below.

Life experiences	Personal beliefs

2 Use your table to answer the following questions:
   a) How might James' beliefs have influenced his decision to go to Spain?
   b What experiences did James have in his life before 1936 that might have influenced his decision?
   c) How would you sum up why James Maley went to fight in Spain?
   d) Revisit your hypothesis from Enquiry Step 2 on page 29. Do you want to make any changes to it?

⬆ Scottish brigade banner.

⬆ James Maley with other Republican prisoners after being captured at the Battle of Jarama (James is on the right-hand side of the front row of the photograph).

James Maley's story

1 19 February 1908. James was born into a poor family in the Calton area of Glasgow. One of a family of nine, he had to leave school early to help his mother, Anne, a hawker, who sold goods from a barrow on the streets of Glasgow. James came from a family of ardent Celtic supporters.

2 In 1929, following the death of his father, he moved to America where he worked briefly in a car factory. He returned to Scotland the next year, homesick and upset by what he saw as the racist attitudes of some Americans towards immigrants. The experience gave James a life-long hatred of racism.

3 In 1932, aged 24, he joined the Communist Party and became a familiar public speaker at Glasgow Green. James was often to be seen speaking from a small portable platform. In his speeches he warned against the dangers of the rise of fascism in Europe. He also attacked the British government for failing to help the poor whose lives were blighted by the poverty and unemployment of the **Great Depression** (see page 64).

4 James was one of 550 volunteers from Scotland (out of a total of 2,300 from the UK) who enlisted with the International Brigades to defend the Spanish Republic during their Civil War. Leaving Glasgow by bus for London, he then travelled to France before being guided over the Pyrenees into Spain. He arrived in Spain in December 1936 and joined the newly formed British Battalion.

5 James first saw action at the Battle of Jarama. He later described shooting until he 'ran out of bullets'. Out of the 500 who advanced towards enemy positions on 12 February 1937, 125 were killed and a similar number injured. James was one of 30 members of the machine-gun company to be captured.

6 Following his arrest James was transferred to a **concentration camp** at Talavera de la Reina, built in the ruins of an old pottery factory just outside Madrid. Here, James and other prisoners were paraded before newsreel cameras. In May 1937, a military court in Salamanca found the men guilty of 'aiding a military rebellion'. James was sentenced to 20 years' imprisonment.

7 James was eventually released from prison as part of a prisoner exchange programme in which captured International Brigade members were released in return for the release of Italian soldiers captured by the Socialists.

8 On his return from Spain, Maley gave in to his mother's pleas for him not to return to the International Brigade, facing certain death if he was recaptured. He continued to speak on public platforms, campaigning for the British government to send help to Spain. In 1941, during the Second World War, he joined the army and served in Burma and India. After the end of the Second World War, he worked as a labourer and continued to speak out against racism and in support of workers' rights. James remained a loyal Celtic football club supporter for the rest of his life.

**Enquiry Step 4:
Concluding your enquiry**

It is time to use the work you have done in Enquiry Steps 1–3 to answer the enquiry question:

Why did James Maley go to Spain in 1936?

In order to communicate your answer, carry out the following activity.

Imagine that you are a television sports commentator watching the 2007 cup-tie between Celtic and St Johnstone. The banners saying 'James Maley R.I.P.' and 'No pasarán' have just been unfurled (see page 28). You need to quickly explain to viewers what is happening. What will you tell them?

Think about explaining:

1 Who was James Maley?

2 What was the Spanish Civil War?

3 What reasons can you give to explain why James decided to go and fight in Spain?

4 What did James do that these supporters might feel proud of?

Did Britain win the Second World War?

During the Second World War, when the bombs were falling and people could have been forgiven for panicking, the government issued a powerfully effective poster: 'Keep Calm and Carry On'. Recently, this has become a popular meme, and – with the benefit of hindsight – you can buy a mug which reassures you: 'Keep Calm, we Won the War'.

But did we? This section will help you decide whether the mug is correct in asserting that Britain won the Second World War.

In May 1940, Hitler's Nazi armies attacked Holland, then swept through Belgium and into France. On 18 June 1940, the British Prime Minister Winston Churchill came before the House of Commons to report that France had surrendered ... but also to convince them that it was now Britain's task to continue the fight to stop the further spread of Nazi fascism. In this speech, Churchill was trying to persuade people that Britain should maintain an 'inflexible resolve to continue the war'.

He concluded:

A

The Battle of France is over. I expect that the Battle of Britain is about to begin. Upon this battle depends the survival of Christian civilization. Upon it depends our own British life...

The whole fury and might of the enemy must very soon be turned on us. Hitler knows that he will have to break us in this Island or lose the war. If we can stand up to him, all Europe may be free and the life of the world may move forward into broad, sunlit uplands. But if we fail, then the whole world, including the United States, including all that we have known and cared for, will sink into the abyss of a new Dark Age...

Let us therefore brace ourselves to our duties, and so bear ourselves that, if the British Empire and its Commonwealth last for a thousand years, men will still say, 'This was their finest hour'.

> **Think**
>
> Study Extract A. Make a list of the words and techniques Churchill uses to persuade and strengthen his listeners.

Background context – war breaks out

It was by no means certain, even in 1939, that Britain would go to war against the Nazis. The 1930s had seen the growth of fascism in Europe (see Section 3) and in Britain (see Section 8). When in the mid-1930s Germany's Nazi leader, Adolf Hitler, adopted an aggressive foreign policy, the British Prime Minister Neville Chamberlain responded with a policy of 'appeasement' which allowed Hitler his 'reasonable' demands.

The diagram below identifies some of the main events on the 'road to war'.

Think

When, in your opinion, did war become unavoidable?

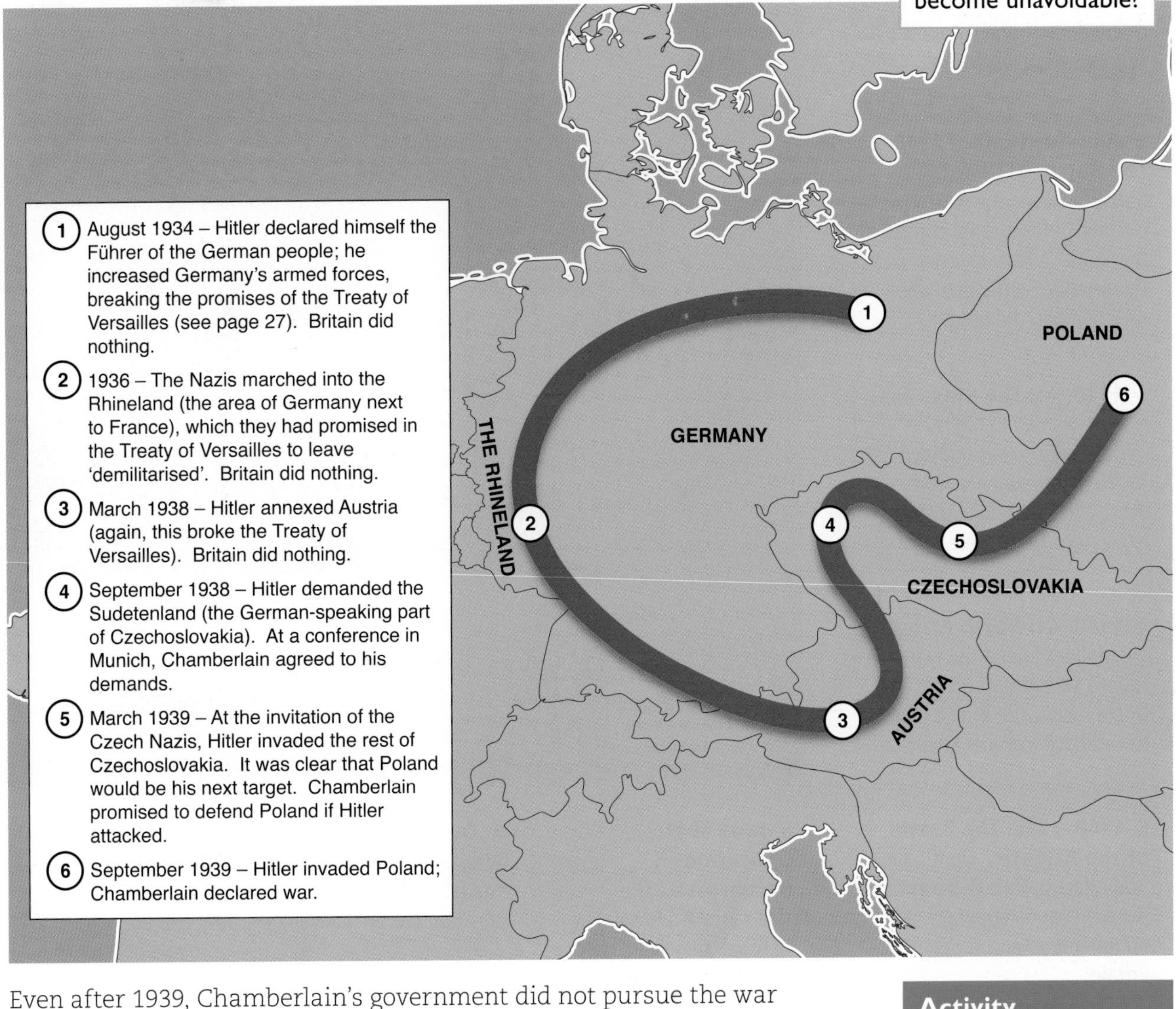

① August 1934 – Hitler declared himself the Führer of the German people; he increased Germany's armed forces, breaking the promises of the Treaty of Versailles (see page 27). Britain did nothing.

② 1936 – The Nazis marched into the Rhineland (the area of Germany next to France), which they had promised in the Treaty of Versailles to leave 'demilitarised'. Britain did nothing.

③ March 1938 – Hitler annexed Austria (again, this broke the Treaty of Versailles). Britain did nothing.

④ September 1938 – Hitler demanded the Sudetenland (the German-speaking part of Czechoslovakia). At a conference in Munich, Chamberlain agreed to his demands.

⑤ March 1939 – At the invitation of the Czech Nazis, Hitler invaded the rest of Czechoslovakia. It was clear that Poland would be his next target. Chamberlain promised to defend Poland if Hitler attacked.

⑥ September 1939 – Hitler invaded Poland; Chamberlain declared war.

Even after 1939, Chamberlain's government did not pursue the war vigorously. Poland fell without the British firing a bullet, and September 1939 to April 1940 was the time of the 'Phoney War', when nothing happened. Some appeasers in Britain secretly plotted to make peace with Hitler.

Then, in April, the Nazis conquered Norway. British attempts to stop them were an embarrassing failure. On 10 May 1940, Chamberlain's government fell, and Churchill became Prime Minister. The Nazis attacked Holland, and swept through Belgium and into France.

Activity

How might the sentiments in Extract A, and the events on this page, have encouraged a feeling after the war that 'Britain won the war'?

The Second World War

This map depicts some of the main events in the Second World War.

1 May–June 1940: Dunkirk. The Nazis swept through Holland and Belgium and invaded France, trapping the British army in Dunkirk – 345,000 men were rescued, but huge amounts of supplies were left behind.

2 July–September 1940: The Battle of Britain. A battle between the RAF and the German Luftwaffe for control of the skies. A Nazi invasion was thwarted in September when the RAF bombed the barges.

3 1940–41: The Blitz. The Nazis switched to night bombing raids. London was bombed for 76 nights running, and other cities (notably Coventry, November 1940) were attacked.

4 1940–41: North Africa. The Italians joined the war on Hitler's side in June 1940. In North Africa, the British were forced back towards Egypt.

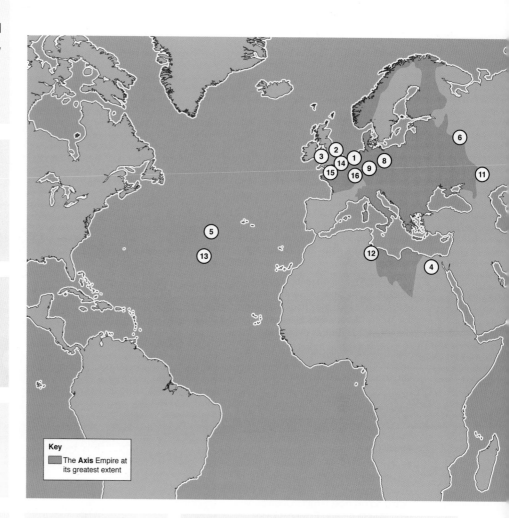

Key
The **Axis** Empire at its greatest extent

5 1940–1945: The Battle of the Atlantic. Hunting in 'Wolf Packs', Nazi **U-boats** sank the merchant shipping that was bringing food and supplies to Britain.

6 June 1941: Operation Barbarossa. The Nazis invaded Russia; by October, they were only 60 miles from Moscow.

7 December 1941: Pearl Harbor. The Japanese attacked the US naval base in the Pacific, bringing the USA into the war. Churchill said that this was the moment he realised he would win the war.

Activity

1 In a 1967 school textbook, the illustrator George Hamilton portrayed the war as a huge 'V' (for victory) – at first nothing but defeats, then a turning point, then nothing but victories. Do you agree with this interpretation of the war? If there was a 'turning point', when was it?

2 Thinking about the events of the war, make a list of the FOUR most important factors which seem to have caused the Allied victory. Write each idea on a separate card.

3 Discuss for each idea HOW that factor would have helped to cause the Allied victory. Write your explanations on the back of the cards. KEEP THE CARDS!

17 August 1945: Hiroshima. The Americans advanced across the Pacific. They faced fierce resistance, especially at Iwo Jima and Okinawa. In August, however, the Americans dropped atomic bombs on Hiroshima (6 August) and Nagasaki (9 August). Japan surrendered.

16 8 May 1945: VE Day (Victory in Europe). The Italians killed Mussolini (28 April) and Hitler committed suicide (30 April). On 2 May Berlin fell to the Russians and on 7 May the Nazis surrendered. Most of Eastern Europe was under Russian control.

15 6 June 1944: D-Day. The British, Americans and Canadians invaded France (much later than the Russians had wanted) and began to fight their way towards Berlin. A Nazi counter-attack (the Battle of the Bulge, December 1944–January 1945) failed to stop their advance.

14 1944: The Baby Blitz. The Nazis fired 9500 V-1 'doodlebug' and 3000 V-2 rockets into Britain.

13 1942: Huff-duff. The British developed a way to work out the U-boats' positions from their radio transmissions; 'hunter-killer' ships sought and sank the U-boat packs.

12 October–November 1942: Battle of El Alamein. The British Eighth Army and American troops defeated the Nazis in North Africa and in July 1943 invaded Italy. Churchill called El Alamein 'the turning point of the war'.

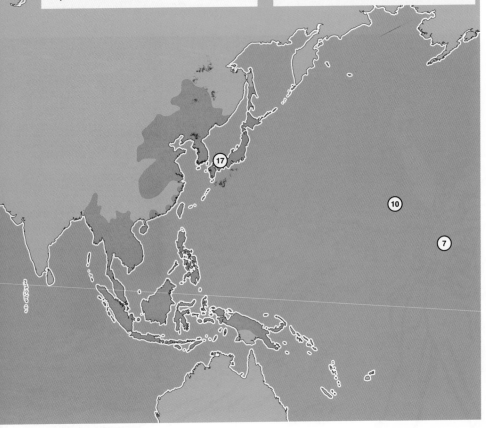

8 Berlin, January 1942: The Wannsee Conference. The Nazis decided to implement their 'final solution' to kill all the Jews in Europe (see pages 46–53). For the rest of the war, vast amounts of money and men were put to this task.

9 1942–45: Bombing Germany. RAF commander 'Bomber' Harris organised huge night-time bombing raids of Germany, including the 'Thousand Bomber Raids' (1942), the 'Dambusters' attack of 1943 and the destruction of Dresden in 1945.

10 June 1942: Midway. After a number of Japanese victories (notable the capture of Singapore in February 1942) the US navy stopped the Japanese at the Battle of Midway.

11 August 1942–January 1943: Battle of Stalingrad. The Russians (and the Russian winter) totally destroyed the German Sixth Army, and the Russian army started to advance towards Berlin. Russian losses were huge (perhaps 25 million dead).

Think

Why might Churchill have identified El Alamein – rather than Stalingrad or Midway – as the turning point of the war?

37

What did the British do to win the war?

After the fall of France in June 1940, the French leader Pétain signed a humiliating armistice which left northern France under military occupation and 'Vichy' France in the south as a puppet Nazi state. In June, also, the Italians entered the war on Hitler's side. For the next year – until Hitler invaded Russia – Britain was left to fight the Nazis alone.

Pages 38–41 describes some of the ways that the British people fought to win the war.

A

" VERY WELL , ALONE "   (Copyright in All Countries.)

Think

1 Study Cartoon A and make a list of its significant elements.
2 Use your list to explain the message of the cartoon.
3 What might someone seeing this cartoon think was the main factor in Germany's eventual defeat?

⬆ This cartoon by David Low for the *Evening Standard*, 18 June 1940, sums up the official version of the British people's attitude to the events of the war at that time. (Low was a British cartoonist who hated Hitler and the Nazis.) By contrast, Ministry of Information surveys of the time, although they found few British people who wanted to surrender, reported many instances of 'pockets of defeatism', grumbling and rumour-spreading.

Adolf Hitler: My Part in His Downfall

'I never believed that [a country] such as ours could ever go to war, let alone win it', commented the comedian Spike Milligan in his memoirs: *Adolf Hitler: My Part in His Downfall*. Yet it did. The British people were at war for six years. It was, moreover, 'total war' – a war which fully engaged the whole nation. For many it involved great sacrifice – for some, the supreme sacrifice. And every one of them – as Milligan's title claimed – played a part in Hitler's defeat.

B

SMILING THROUGH: Exhibit 2862
"Do I **Mend**, or **Make-do** with this? I'm referring, of course, to the garment."

Think

1 Study Cartoon B and make a list of the significant elements of the scene.
2 Use your list to explain the message of the cartoon.
3 What might someone seeing this cartoon think was the main factor in Germany's eventual defeat?

Evacuation: to protect children from the effects of German bombing raids, 827,000 children, 524,000 mothers-with-babies, and 103,000 teachers (to look after them) were evacuated to the countryside.

Rationing: With food and supplies endangered by Nazi U-Boats, the government issued Ration Books (for goods such as petrol, butter, sugar, paper, meat and clothing), and passed laws to force tailors to make 'utility' clothing which used less material. A daily radio programme – 'The Kitchen Front' – gave tips on how to make tasty meals out of the limited foodstuffs available. Gardeners were encouraged to 'Dig for Victory' and to 'Grow Your Own'. Housewives tried to 'Make Do and Mend'. The campaign was a great success; during the war, despite the shortages, the population was healthier than it had ever been.

◀ This 'Smiling Through' cartoon by Joseph Lee appeared in the *Evening News* on 19 November 1943.

Activity

1 Working in a small group, use the information on pages 39–41 to find the FOUR most important reasons why the people of Britain came successfully through the war. Write each idea on a separate card.
2 Discuss for each idea HOW that factor would have helped Britain to win the war. Write your explanations on the back of the cards. KEEP THE CARDS!

Dunkirk evacuation: with the British army trapped at Dunkirk in France in May 1940, while churchgoers held a day of prayer for calm seas, an armada of volunteers – fishing boats, yachts, paddle steamers – sailed across the Channel to pick up soldiers from the beaches. It was a propaganda triumph – Churchill called it 'a miracle of deliverance'.

Enigma: working in Bletchley Park, Alan Turing and his team invented Enigma (this would later be called the computer) to decode the Nazis' radio communications. The Nazis never realised their code was broken, and it has been suggested that Turing's work shortened the war by two years.

C

⬆ This cartoon by Leslie Gilbert Illingworth was published in the *Daily Mail* on 17 September 1940 – two days after a huge daytime attack by the Nazi Luftwaffe had failed (the RAF claimed it had shot down 187 German planes).

Battle of Britain: during 1940–41 – the years when Britain alone was fighting the Nazis, the Spitfires and Hurricanes of the RAF – together with the newly developed radar stations – defeated the German Luftwaffe. Without air superiority, the Nazis dared not launch an invasion across the English Channel. In August 1940, Churchill claimed the fighter pilots were 'turning the tide of the world war by their prowess and by their devotion. Never in the field of human conflict was so much owed by so many to so few.'

HF/DF: 'Huff-duff' was the technique of using radio waves and a double antenna to triangulate the location of the sender. During the war it was improved and, after 1942, the Admiralty Signal Establishment worked out how to use it on ships – a development which helped The Royal Navy to find and destroy the Nazi U-Boats.

Think

1 Study Cartoon C and make a list of the significant elements of the scene.
2 Use your list to explain the message of the cartoon.
3 What might someone seeing this cartoon think was the main factor in Germany's eventual defeat?

ARP: the British reaction to the Blitz was not just a man shouting 'Put that light out'. It involved:

- 38 million gas masks
- Anderson and Morrison bomb shelters
- sleeping in the Tube
- the Auxiliary Fire and Ambulance Services
- 27,000 volunteers in the Royal Observer Corps who stayed up all night listening for German planes;
- the Women's Voluntary Service who set up tea canteens, looked after victims, helped with First Aid and manned Incident Enquiry posts.

The British did not behave as wonderfully as the propaganda suggested, but they 'kept calm and carried on'.

Home Guard: was not as chaotic as the 1970s TV series *Dad's Army* portrayed. Numbering 1.5 million men, they guarded the coast, and defended strategic military sites. Some manned anti-aircraft guns, and elite Auxiliary Units were trained to carry on a guerrilla resistance if the Nazis invaded.

The **Political Warfare Executive:** carried out 'black propaganda' designed to damage German morale, dropping anti-Nazi leaflets, and running a bogus 'German' radio programme criticising Hitler.

Government propaganda: all the media were strictly censored. Newspapers were carefully controlled and did not carry any news or photographs which would damage morale. Posters carried government messages. The writer J.B. Priestley gave his motivational 'Postscripts' talks on the radio. The film of Shakespeare's *Henry V* reminded people of the heroism of the 'happy few' who fought at Agincourt in 1415.

Britain's Women: from 1941, single women aged 20–30 could be **conscripted** into the armed forces or into industry. Some women – such as the 'Aycliffe Angels' of County Durham – did hugely dangerous work filling shells in the Royal Ordnance Factories. About 80,000 girls joined the Women's Land Army to help farmers.

Military service: nearly 3.5 million men and 487,000 women were conscripted or volunteered to serve in the armed forces during the war; 383,700 were killed. Others suffered horrific wounds or conditions (such as those who were captured by the Japanese, or were on the Arctic convoys).

Internment: by the summer of 1940, the 60,000 Germans and Austrians who lived in Britain (including, ironically, both Nazis and Jews fleeing the Nazis) had been interned (rounded up and imprisoned) because they were felt to be a security risk. When Italy entered the war, all 15,000 Italians living in Britain were arrested.

⬆ This cartoon by the British cartoonist Leslie Gilbert Illingworth appeared in the *Daily Mail* on 28 August 1944, and shows the story of the war from the British point of view, 1940–44. Can you spot: trying on gas masks, Dunkirk, the Home Guard, the Battle of Britain, the Blitz, evacuation, rationing and war work?

Why did Germany lose the war?

If we are properly to evaluate Britain's role in winning the war, we will need to look at the other factors involved in defeat of the Nazis. Pages 42–44 look at a selection of suggestions people have made. You will see that, on this topic, writers' opinions have changed over time:

- During the war, people understandably tended to explain victory simply in terms of military might – bigger armies, better strategies.
- After 1945, a Cold War developed between the Soviet Union and Britain and America. Western historians did not have access to Russian war records, so they tended to place more emphasis on the role played by Britain and America.
- In 1991, the Soviet Union collapsed, and modern historians – with access to the Soviet war records – now often emphasise the role played by the Soviet Union.

A

↑ This cartoon by Leslie Gilbert Illingworth appeared in the *Daily Mail* on 17 July 1944, as the Soviet Army was driving the Nazis out of the Soviet Union. The sign on the table reads: 'Space reserved for lion skin'.

> **Think**
>
> 1 Study Cartoon A and identify the significant elements:
>   a) What does the bear represent?
>   b) Which country is often represented by a lion?
> 2 Explain the message of the cartoon.
> 3 What did this cartoon suggest was the main cause of Germany's defeat?

B

⬆ This cartoon by Sidney 'George' Strube appeared in the *Daily Express* on 2 April 1945, a month before the Nazi surrender. The uniforms of the soldiers on the left identify them as Soviets (advancing from the east). The soldiers on the right are British and Americans (attacking from the west).

Think

1 Study Cartoon B and identify the significant elements.
2 Explain the message of the cartoon.
3 What did this cartoon suggest was the main cause of Germany's defeat?

C

Three factors defeated us in the West where I was in command.

First, the unheard-of superiority of your air force, which made all movement in daytime impossible.

Second, the lack of motor fuel oil and gas – so that the Panzers and even the remaining Luftwaffe were unable to move.

Third, the systematic destruction of all railway communications so that it was impossible to bring one single railroad train across the Rhine. This made impossible the reshuffling of troops and robbed us of all mobility.

The Nazi General Feldmarschall Karl Gerd von Rundstedt, speaking to Allied interrogators in 1945.

D

WHY DID THE AXIS POWERS LOSE THE WAR?

a. A basic weakness was shortage of raw materials.

b. The Allies soon learned from their early failures.

c. The Nazis simply took on too much.

d. The combined resources of the Americans and the Russians, not to mention the British empire.

e. The Nazis made serious tactical mistakes.

Norman Lowe, *Mastering Modern World History* – a GCSE revision book, 1982.

↑ The 1970 Hollywood blockbuster *Patton* starts with actor George C Scott – as controversial US general George S Patton – delivering an inspiring speech to his soldiers. It then shows him reviving flagging Allied morale, winning the war in North Africa, and driving the Nazis back across Europe after D-Day. The film also shows him insulting Russian soldiers and prophesying that, after the war, Britain and America would be the world superpowers.

Think

1 Study film still E and identify the significant elements.
2 Explain the message of the film.
3 What did this image suggest was the main cause of Germany's defeat?

F

Three broad explanations of Germany's defeat have been suggested:

– A resources shortfall – Germany attempted to wage too much war with too few assets.

– The hideous nature of the regime and the personality and beliefs of its all-powerful leader.

– Errors in statecraft, military strategy and operational direction.

War, Peace and International Relations (2007), written by Colin S Gray, the British-American Professor of Strategic Studies at the University of Reading.

G

Statistically, the Eastern Front was where the war was won – out of every five Germans killed in battlefield combat, four died on the Eastern Front. Yes, the British and Americans smashed Germany's war economy and defeated the Luftwaffe and *Kriegsmarine*; but when it came to killing Germans on the ground, the Russians were far and away more effective.

The British historian, journalist and Second World War expert Andrew Roberts, speaking to HistoryNet in 2011.

Activity

1 Working in a small group, use the information on pages 42–44 to find the EIGHT most important reasons given in evidence A–G for Germany's defeat. Write each idea on a separate card.
2 Discuss for each idea HOW that factor would have caused Germany's defeat in the war. Write your explanations on the back of the cards.
3 Evaluate the reliability of each suggestion. Consider issues such as:
   ▌ Provenance – e.g. who made the suggestion and how much of an authority are they?
   ▌ Motive – e.g. what were they trying to achieve and did they have a motive to deceive?
   ▌ Date – e.g. were they there at the time or, if not, is it the latest research?

When you have considered each suggestion, write 'unreliable', 'reliable' or 'very reliable' across each card as appropriate.

Concluding your study

Now you are in a position to be able to answer the enquiry question:
Did Britain win the Second World War?

Activity

From your work on pages 36, 39 and 44, you should have 16 cards with explained reasons why the Nazis failed to win the Second World War.

1 Rank the cards into an order of impact, with the most effective cause on the top, and the least effective at the bottom. Take account of your explanation of how the cause worked to win the war, but also of the historical authority of the people suggesting it. Use this ranking to write an 'impact' score on each card, from 16 for the most crucial factor of all, to 1 for the cause you decided was least important. An example is given below.

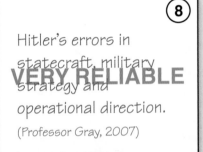

Hitler's errors in statecraft, military strategy and operational direction.
(Professor Gray, 2007)

⑧

VERY RELIABLE

As Hitler made more and more mistakes, the Allies were able to recover, take advantage and defeat him – he defeated himself.

2 Identify all the cards which ascribe a role to the British in the Allied victory:
   a) Where do these ideas rank in your order of importance?
   b) How reliable as historical authorities are the people suggesting the ideas?
   c) Taking the cards together, how do they compare to the factors in which Britain was *not* involved?

3 You should now be able, as a whole class, to have a discussion of the issue: 'Did Britain win the Second World War?'

4 Draw your own design for a 'Keep Calm' mug which sums up the part Britain played in the Second World War. Prepare an argument to justify your design, explaining:
   ■ What part Britain played in the Allied victory in the Second World War.
   ■ What other factors were involved in the Allied victory.
   ■ Whether it is correct to say 'We Won the War' and why your design is the correct interpretation.

How did anti-Semitism change over time?

The Holocaust is the name given to the killing of 6 million Jewish people by the Nazis during the Second World War (see pages 48–49). However, Hitler and his Nazi Party did not invent **anti-Semitism**. In this section you will explore the roots of anti-Semitism before looking at the development of the Holocaust and Jewish attempts at resistance.

0AD

The Romans

In AD 70, the Romans forced the Jews to leave their homeland. The Jews settled in North Africa, Spain, and eastern and western Europe. Over the next few centuries, many Jews mixed with their Christian and Muslim neighbours, while others lived separately in order to preserve their culture, language and beliefs.

Early Christian leaders blamed the Jews for the death of Jesus. Some Christian communities drove out Jews and seized their land, homes and belongings.

500AD

The Middle Ages

During the **Crusades**, Christian armies on their way to the Holy Land also attacked and destroyed Jewish communities. The Jews were blamed for the death of Christ and for not accepting Christianity.

In the twelfth century, a lie began to circulate in Europe that Jews stole and killed Christian children to use their blood for making **Passover** bread. Jews were likely to be **segregated** in **ghettos**, while others were forced to leave altogether. Jews were expelled from England in 1290, from France in 1394 and Spain in 1492. During the Black Death (1348–51), thousands of Jews in Europe were attacked and murdered after being wrongly blamed for poisoning the wells and causing the sickness. This violence was particularly widespread in the states that later formed Germany and many Jews fled to Poland.

1000AD

The late nineteenth-century

Towards the end of the nineteenth century, there were outbreaks of anti-Semitic violence in Russia, causing many Jews to move to safety in Europe. However, new ideas were appearing that argued people could be divided into a hierarchy of different races. Some went further, saying Jews were inferior and posed a threat to the racial 'purity' of a nation. In Austria and Germany these ideas were influenced by the belief that the Germanic race was superior to all others. Some newspaper editors, politicians and even musicians like Richard Wagner presented anti-Semitic ideas to the German public.

1500AD

Weimar Germany

The Jews who fled Russia and settled in Germany in the 1890s quickly became valuable members of society. Many considered themselves Germans first and Jews second, joining the army and fighting for Germany during the First World War. Even though Jews made up less than one per cent of the German population, many contributed to society as doctors, lawyers and other professions. However, defeat in the First World War and the economic problems facing Germany in the Weimar period were sometimes blamed on the Jews.

2000AD

A

◀ Carving showing Roman soldiers looting the Jewish temple in Jerusalem.

B

In Christian Europe, Jews were not allowed to own land or learn a trade and so had few ways to make a living. Some ran successful businesses while others became money lenders (an occupation the Church banned Christians from doing) to make ends meet. This often led to envy and bad feeling towards Jews.

⬆ German Jews being burnt in fifteenth-century Germany.

C

The Nazis did not discard the past; they built on it. They did not begin a development; they completed it.

Raul Hilberg, Holocaust Historian, 1961.

Activity

1 Using the timeline and Evidence B and C, make a list of all of the accusations made against Jews over time.
2 Persecution often develops when a person or a group of people is regarded as different to others. In what ways have Jewish communities been seen as different in the past?
3 How was anti-Semitism in the nineteenth century different to that of earlier periods?
4 As you work through the rest of this section, think how far you agree with Extract A (above). What similarities and differences can you find between Nazi treatment of the Jews and earlier anti-Semitism?

5

How did the Holocaust happen and in what ways was it resisted?

A straight or twisted path?
Was the Holocaust inevitable in 1933?

Adolf Hitler became Chancellor of Germany in 1933 (see page 49). By the time of his suicide in 1945, 6 million of Europe's Jews had been killed. Most died in purpose-built death camps in eastern Europe. The Nazis constructed gas chambers that could hold 2,000 people at once and used Europe's rail network to transport Jews to killing centres at Chelmno, Treblinka, Sobibor, Majdanek and Belzec. However, the most notorious of the extermination camps was Auschwitz, where over 1 million Jews were killed.

Historians agree that Hitler's vicious anti-Semitic ideas were the driving force behind the Holocaust. However, they disagree over whether the Holocaust was inevitable (bound to happen) the moment Hitler came to power in 1933. The different arguments are outlined in Diagram B on page 49. In this chapter, you will investigate how events unfolded before reaching your own conclusion to the enquiry question: **A straight or twisted path? Was the Holocaust inevitable in 1933?**

A

⬆ The railway line leading into the main gate at Auschwitz. The sign on the gate said 'Arbeit macht frei' meaning 'Work brings freedom'. However, the Jews who arrived at the camp had no chance of release.

Think

The Nazis sometimes decorated the arrival areas in the death camps with potted flowers and signs like the one mentioned in the caption to Picture A. Why do you think they did this?

B

Hitler's actions at home and abroad were driven by his determination to purify and strengthen the German race. Jews were seen as a threat to be rooted out and removed. The Holocaust was the final phase of a long-held plan. Therefore, the 'road to Auschwitz' was a 'straight' path and inevitable once Hitler came to power.

The Holocaust was not part of a long-held plan and was not inevitable when Hitler came to power in 1933. Instead, it was more of an improvised attempt to deal with an increasing number of Jews under Nazi control. Hitler definitely approved of the actions taken against the Jews but the plan emerged bit by bit. Therefore, the 'road to Auschwitz' was a 'twisted' path.

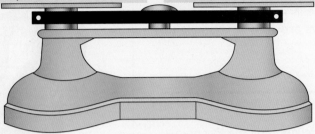

← The historical debate.

C

Hitler believed that world history was determined by a struggle between races. The Aryan (German) race was locked in a permanent conflict with the Jews, who he described as a 'racial tuberculosis among nations'. He argued Germany needed a strong government whose aim should be 'the removal of Jews altogether'.

One of Hitler's aims was to win more living space in Eastern Europe at the expense of Poland and the Soviet Union. He regarded the Slavs that lived there as an inferior race to be pushed aside.

Hitler believed that after the First World War, the German army had been 'stabbed in the back' by weak politicians, Communists and Jews. He blamed Jews for defeat in the First World War (see page 26).

Hitler blamed Jews for inventing communism and controlling the Soviet Union, as Karl Marx had been a Jew and many of Russia's early revolutionaries had themselves been Jewish. At the same time, he also accused Jews of controlling big business.

↑ Hitler's anti-Semitic ideas in 1933.

Enquiry Step 1: First evidence – asking questions

1 After reading Hitler's ideas in C, do they suggest the Holocaust was inevitable when he came to power in 1933? Explain your thinking.

2 Why is it so difficult to be sure at this stage of your investigation? What else would you need to know to come to a firm conclusion?

Nazi treatment of the Jews 1933–45 (part 1)

The evidence and information on these pages will give you some idea about how the Nazis treated the Jews in Germany and the countries they occupied during the Second World War. This will help you investigate whether the Holocaust was inevitable when Hitler came to power in 1933.

Enquiry Step 2: Suggesting an answer

1 Read pages 50–51. Add as many details as you can to your own copy of the timeline below. We have provided an example to help get you started.

April 1933, boycott of Jewish businesses and shops

▼

1933 1934 1935 1936 1937 1938 1939 1940 1941 1942 1943 1944 1945

2 Colour code the events on your timeline using the key below. You may need to underline some events in more than one colour. Don't worry if you do not use all of the colours, there is more evidence on pages 52–53.

Propaganda   Segregation (separation)   Emigration

Violence   Mass extermination

3 Based on your investigation *so far*, was the Holocaust inevitable as soon as Hitler came to power in 1933? Explain your thinking and compare your ideas to those of others in your class.

4 Coming together as a whole class, compare your timelines so far.
   a) Discuss what patterns you notice. Use your colour coding to help you.
   b) Is it possible at this point to identify any turning points in the Nazi treatment of the Jews?
   c) Is it possible yet to suggest a point at which the Holocaust became 'inevitable'?

D

GROSSE POLITISCHE SCHAU IM BIBLIOTHEKSBAU DES DEUTSCHEN MUSEUMS ZU MÜNCHEN · AB 8. NOVEMBER 1937 · TÄGLICH GEÖFFNET VON 10-21 UHR

⬆ The poster for the Eternal Jew exhibition, 1937.

The Eternal Jew exhibition encouraged Germans to regard Jews as foreigners and 'alien' to the rest of society. It also attempted to 'expose' a worldwide Jewish–Communist conspiracy. The exhibition attracted 412,300 visitors, over 5,000 per day.

E

In 1940, Jews living in Nazi-controlled Poland were ordered into ghettos. These were areas within cities separated by walls and armed guards. In the Warsaw ghetto, an average of six people lived in just one room. The Nazis restricted food supplies so hunger and starvation were common. Anyone trying to leave the ghetto or smuggle food in was shot.

⬅ Starving children in the Warsaw ghetto, 1941.

F

← A Nazi stormtrooper watches a burning synagogue during *Kristallnacht* (night of broken glass), 9–10 November 1938. Many Jewish shop windows were smashed, giving the event its name. Nazis attacked hundreds of Jewish shops, businesses and synagogues in Germany. Over 90 Jews were killed in the violence. In the same month, Jews were banned from running businesses. Jewish children were no longer allowed to attend state schools.

G

German Foreign Ministry Memo from July 1940, describing a plan to deport all Jews under German rule to the French colony of Madagascar, 400 km off the south-east coast of Africa. The Nazis thought many would die on the journey or from the inhospitable climate once they got there. However, the plan was never carried out, as Germany could not control the sea routes to Africa.

The imminent victory [France had been defeated and Germany was expecting Britain to surrender] gives Germans the possibility of solving the Jewish question in Europe. The desirable solution is: All Jews out of Europe… in the peace treaty, France must make the island of Madagascar available.

H

← Nazi stormtroopers carry signs saying, 'Germans! Defend yourselves! Do not buy from Jews!' In April 1933, Hitler ordered a boycott of Jewish shops and businesses. In the same month, Jewish teachers were banned from teaching in state schools and Jewish civil servants were sacked. Jews were excluded from sports clubs and Jewish children were forbidden to play with Aryan children. A month earlier, Jews were banned from working as lawyers or judges.

I

↑ A couple are forced to wear signs saying, 'I am the greatest pig and only let Jews in' and 'As a young Jew, I only take German girls into my room'.

In 1935, Hitler passed the Nuremberg Laws. Marriages and sexual relationships between Jews and Germans were banned. Jews were forbidden to display the national flag or employ female citizens under 45 years old. All German Jews lost their rights as citizens.

51

Nazi treatment of the Jews 1933–45 (part 2)

5

How did the Holocaust happen and in what ways was it resisted?

Enquiry Step 3: Developing your answer

1 Using the evidence on these two pages, continue adding to the timeline you started in Enquiry Step 2 on page 50.
2 Colour code events using the same key (propaganda; segregation; emigration; violence; mass extermination).
3 Coming together as a whole class, compare your timelines.
   a) Discuss what patterns you notice. Use your colour coding to help you.
   b) Can you identify any turning points in the Nazi treatment of the Jews?
   c) Is it possible to suggest a point where the Holocaust became 'inevitable'?

J

The Wansee Conference of January 1942 was a meeting of leading Nazis to agree a plan to round up and 'resettle' Europe's 11 million Jews in the east. However, those attending the conference knew that resettlement meant extermination. Following the conference, plans to build death camps complete with gas chambers and crematoria were put into action.

K

Special squads called **Einsatzgruppen** were sent into eastern Europe following the German army's invasion of Poland, and then into the Soviet Union (see pages 36–7). They rounded up local Jews and shot them, before burying them in mass graves. Approximately 2 million Jews were killed this way between 1941 and 1945.

L

↑ Jews arriving at Auschwitz, c.1942.

By spring 1942, gassing was the main method used for killing Jews. It is estimated over 4 million Jews (plus Gypsies, homosexuals and Jehovah's Witnesses) perished in the extermination camps. Some death camps used a number of Jews as slave labour to support the German war effort. These Jews were also killed once they ceased to be 'useful'.

↑ Members of an *Einsatzgruppen* (mobile killing squad) conduct a mass shooting of Jews, Ukraine, Summer 1941.

M

⬆ German youths reading the Nazi-controlled newspaper, *Der Stürmer*, 1933. This violently anti-Semitic paper was publicly displayed from 1933 to 1945. It stereotyped Jews, showing them with coarse features and black hair, in contrast to blond-haired and blue-eyed Aryans.

N

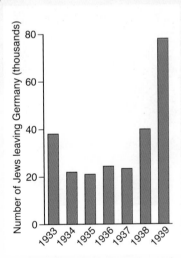

⬆ The Nazis encouraged Jewish emigration by 'every possible means'. However, virtually all property was confiscated before Jews were allowed to leave the country. There was also a limit to the number of Jews other countries would admit.

Enquiry Step 4: Concluding your enquiry

1 Mark the following events on your timeline.

September 1939: The *Second World War* began. Germany rapidly conquered Poland. 1.7 million Polish Jews fell under Nazi control, along with the 230,000 Jews still living in Germany. These extra Jews were regarded as subhuman and were separated from the rest of society.

June 1941: Hitler launched *Operation Barbarossa*, the invasion of the Soviet Union. Around 2 million more Jews fell under Nazi control. Hitler told his commanders that this was to be a war of extermination. The Nazi leadership planned in advance the death by starvation of 30 million Slavs to create 'living space' for Germans.

▮ Do they help to explain the turning points you identified in Enquiry Step 3?

2 Working in pairs or small groups, use your completed timelines and the information on pages 50–3 to complete your own copy of the grid below. Make sure that you use supporting evidence to support or challenge each statement.

Statement	Agree/ Disagree	Evidence to support or challenge
1 Hitler had strong anti-Semitic feelings even before he became leader of Germany.		
2 The persecution of Jews got worse over time.		
3 Following the invasion of Poland in September 1939, the Nazis were already planning to kill all Jews under their control.		
4 The invasion of the USSR in June 1941 was a turning point in the treatment of Jews. After this plans were put in place for the mass extermination of all of Europe's Jews.		

3 Look back at the historical debate (B) on page 49. Which interpretation – (A) straight-path or (B) twisted-path – do you most agree with? Use your completed timeline and grid to explain your reasons.

OR

4 Suggest your own interpretation, using your completed timeline and grid to explain your reasons.
   a) Think about the patterns that your colour coding reveals. How did treatment of the Jews change over time?
   b) Was the Holocaust inevitable when Hitler came to power in 1933 or did it become inevitable at a later date? Explain your thinking.

5

How did the Holocaust happen and in what ways was it resisted?

What would you include in a memorial to Jewish resistance?

You have already explored the development of the Holocaust and developed a detailed picture of the horrors committed by the Nazis. On pages 54–61 we turn our attention to the different reactions of Jewish people caught up in the middle of these terrible events.

> **Think**
>
> Photographs A–D show Jews during the Holocaust. Which is the odd one out? Discuss your reasons.

⬆ Jewish women and children being led naked to the gas chambers at Treblinka, c.1942.

⬆ Jewish women on the train to Auschwitz.

⬆ Jewish partisans (resistance fighters in German-held territory) in Vilna, 1944.

Photographs A, B and D regularly appear in school textbooks but images like C are rarely seen. Television documentaries often feature similar images that can give the misleading and disrespectful impression that Jews went like sheep to the slaughter. In fact, given the obstacles they faced (see page 55), there *was* a surprising amount of Jewish resistance to the Nazis. This took many forms, not all of them obvious.

⬅ German soldiers round up Jews in the Warsaw ghetto for removal to a death camp, 1943.

Obstacles to resistance

A number of key factors made any resistance to the Nazis both difficult and dangerous in occupied Europe. These problems were even more acute for Jews.

E

We had no weapons except for rocks, bottles and a few knives. We were completely outnumbered and surrounded by a trained German military force supported loyally by the local population. But then again, we had no expectation that we would live beyond the next few weeks or months. Why not resist when the alternative was death at a time or place chosen by the Nazis? Desperation was what drove us, along with the desire for revenge. Our families had been butchered and piled into nameless graves. The thought of taking a few German lives in return was a powerful incentive.

Izik Sutin, a Polish Jew, describing some of the problems facing Jews who chose to resist, 1942.

F

If an individual resisted, their whole family or community were punished. If a Jew in a ghetto or camp broke the rules it could lead to the punishment of many others.

Jews faced enormous difficulty finding hiding places to avoid being sent to a ghetto or camp. Food was scarce and the local population was not always willing to help. Those that did help Jews risked the death penalty.

The Nazis kept the shootings and death camps secret for as long as possible. The first Jews arriving at Auschwitz were forced to write postcards telling friends and family that they had arrived and were well. Then they were gassed.

The German army rapidly conquered Poland in 1939 and took just six weeks to defeat France in 1940. It was incredibly difficult for mostly unarmed civilians to resist this well-trained fighting force.

⬆ The execution of Jewish partisans, Minsk, October 1941.

Activity

1 Read this page. Which was the biggest obstacle preventing Jewish resistance?
2 Can you think of any other possible obstacles to resistance not mentioned here?

5

How did the Holocaust happen and in what ways was it resisted?

On page 55, you considered the obstacles facing Jews in resisting the Nazis. However, Jewish resistance did occur even in the most difficult of situations. In the activity below you will consider the different ways that Jews attempted to resist during the Holocaust.

Your task is to use the information on pages 56–61 to identify and describe all of the ways that Jewish people resisted the terrible situation they found themselves in. Then you will consider which types of resistance were the most common and explain the reasons for this. Finally, you will use your understanding to design your own memorial to Jewish resistance.

The information you will look at focuses on three different areas:

- Resistance in the ghettos (pages 56–58)
- Resistance in occupied Europe (pages 59–60)
- Resistance in the camps (pages 60–61).

Resistance in the ghettos

Between 1939 and 1943, hundreds of thousands of Jews were forced into more than 400 ghettos in eastern Europe. Here they were isolated from the outside world by walls and barbed wire. Starvation and disease killed tens of thousands and weakened those who survived. Despite this, there were armed uprisings in five of the major ghettos and 45 smaller ghettos in eastern Europe. There were also numerous examples of day-to-day resistance as shown in the illustrations on page 57..

Activity

1 Historians have identified different types of resistance. These are:
   (i) Direct resistance – actions taken *against* the enemy (the Nazis).
   (ii) Indirect resistance – actions taken *in support* of the oppressed (the Jews).
   (iii) Active resistance – doing something to disrupt the enemy's goals.
   (iv) Passive resistance – a refusal to act or not doing what the enemy wants.
   Make your own large copy of the table below so that you can start to identify different examples of Jewish resistance.

2 Use the information on pages 56–61 to find as many examples of Jewish resistance as you can. Write each one on a sticky note or slip of paper. Stick or place the examples you have collected on your own copy of the table. We have provided one for you as an example in the table below.

	Active resistance	Passive resistance
Direct resistance		
Indirect resistance		Secret political groups were formed in ghettos. Helped feed people and were a front for secret meetings.

Underground political parties and groups

Secret political groups were formed. At first, these focused on helping other Jews within the ghetto. Soup kitchens helped feed people and often served as a front for secret meetings.

Underground newspapers and radios

Illegal newspapers were published in the larger ghettos and were good for morale. Some listened to foreign stations on smuggled radios; this made people feel less isolated and kept them up to date with events in the war.

Acts of sabotage

Some Jews were used as forced labourers in or near the ghettos. They could damage factory machinery, slow production, steal parts, set fires and deliberately produce faulty munitions.

Couriers

Jewish couriers (messengers who had avoided being rounded up) carried illegal newspapers, money, forged papers and information between the ghettos. Some smuggled in weapons and helped arrange escapes. A secret communication network was established between the ghettos of Eastern Europe. In Extract G (below), one courier tells of her experiences and the risks involved.

G

The main objective of our mission on the 'Aryan side' – the goal for which we endured constant danger, hid like frightened animals, assumed false identities, moved from dwelling to dwelling to escape detection as Jews – was to obtain arms for resistance in the ghetto. Yurek had succeeded in buying a considerable amount of revolvers and hand grenades...the **Gestapo** swooped down on him. Several months later I learned Yurek had been tortured by the Gestapo. His hands and toes had been beaten to a pulp, yet he had not betrayed his co-workers.

Vladka Meed, a Jewish courier.

5

How did the Holocaust happen and in what ways was it resisted?

Armed uprisings in the ghettos

When couriers first brought the news of mass shootings and extermination camps to the ghettos, the majority of Jews simply did not or could not believe what they were hearing. It was not until the Nazis started destroying the ghettos and sending Jews to the extermination camps that armed resistance broke out. Most Jews who resisted were realistic about their low chances of success, but wanted to die fighting and choose their own manner of death.

In April 1943, and after most of the ghetto had been sent to the death camps, Jewish fighters fired on German soldiers. The fighters moved around using a network of cellars, rooftops and bunkers.

Around 750 Jewish men and women, armed with a few rifles, pistols and homemade petrol bombs, held on for 28 days against 2,000 German troops. Only after fierce house-to-house fighting did the Germans recapture the ghetto; 56,000 Jews were rounded up and 7,000 of them were shot.

The rest were deported to extermination or labour camps. Some were able to escape, and a number joined the Polish Resistance (a secret organisation of Poles who attempted to disrupt the Nazi war effort) or helped other Jews to hide.

⬇ German soldiers patrol a burning street during the Warsaw ghetto uprising, 1943.

H

Resistance in Occupied Europe

Historians have estimated that between 20,000 and 30,000 Jews fought in partisan (resistance fighters) groups in the forested areas of eastern Europe. This was an incredibly risky business as Jews were as much at risk from other partisan groups as from the German army. Many partisans hated the Jews just as much as they hated the Nazis. Some Jews fighting in non-Jewish partisan units kept their identity secret.

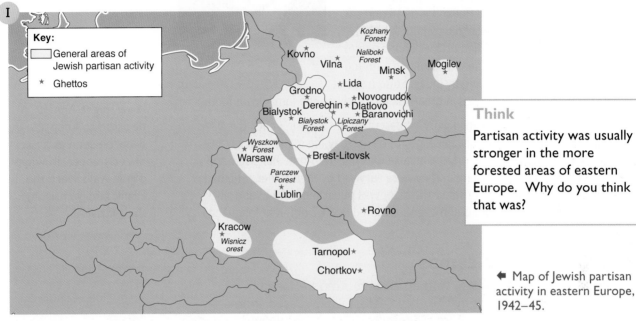

← Map of Jewish partisan activity in eastern Europe, 1942–45.

Think

Partisan activity was usually stronger in the more forested areas of eastern Europe. Why do you think that was?

Partisan units waged a hit-and-run campaign against the German army, attacking supply lines and disrupting the war effort. They sabotaged railways and bridges. Most partisans were single, able-bodied men. However, some Jewish fighters also welcomed women, children and the elderly who had escaped from the ghettos. It is estimated that around 10,000 Jews survived the war by joining such groups.

Don't rush to fight and die. So few of us are left, we need to save lives. It is more important to save Jews than to kill Germans.

Tuvia Bielski

The Bielski brothers ran a family camp in the Naliboki forest in Poland. The group accepted all Jews, regardless of age, sex or ability to fight.

Scouts ranged the surrounding forests on the lookout for other escaped Jews who they could bring to their camp.

The group was started in 1942 and numbered fewer than 40 people. However, by the summer of 1944 an estimated 1,200 Jews had joined them.

The brothers sent special scouts into the ghettos to rescue Jews who would then join the group hiding in the forest.

← Members of the Bielski family camp, 1944.

5

How did the Holocaust happen and in what ways was it resisted?

Anne Frank (1929–1945)

Many of you will have already heard of Anne Frank, but it is worth considering how her actions and the actions of others like her might be regarded as examples of Jewish resistance.

K

Anne was born in Germany, but in 1933 her family moved to Holland to escape the discrimination of the Nazis. Germany invaded Holland in 1940 and all Jews were forced to wear a yellow star. In July 1942, Anne's sister Margot was called up for deportation to a work camp. This caused the Franks, along with four other families, to go into hiding by moving into a secret annexe. Friends put themselves at great risk by supplying the family with food.

⬆ Anne Frank c.1940.

While in hiding Anne kept a vivid diary. It described the ways in which the Nazis persecuted Dutch Jews and the challenges of day-to-day life in the annexe. In 1944, after an anonymous tip off, the annexe was raided. Anne, her sister and her mother all died in Nazi camps. They were survived by their father, who had managed to keep Anne's diary safe. The diary was published in 1947 and since then has sold millions of copies and been translated into 67 different languages.

Think

How might Anne's decision to keep a diary be seen as an act of resistance? In what other ways were the Frank family resisting the Nazis?

Resistance in the camps

At least 4 million Jewish men, women and children perished in extermination camps built by the Nazis. Most were gassed soon after arrival, while the physically fit were temporarily kept alive and forced to work. Barbed wire, guard towers and electrified fences meant that there was very little chance of escape. Camp inmates were punished harshly for breaking the rules and the Nazis carried out frequent roll calls to count the prisoners.

Camp guards temporarily spared a small number of Jewish prisoners for use in small units called **Sonderkommandos**. These were responsible for operating the crematoria and other facilities in the camps. This meant staying alive a little longer, but *Sonderkommandos* knew that it was only a matter of time before they too would be gassed.

L

◀ A photograph, secretly taken by a *Sonderkommando*, showing bodies being burnt at Auschwitz, 1944.

Think

1 Why might taking such photographs be considered an act of resistance?
2 What do you think the photographer was trying to achieve?

Most organised resistance in the camps was aimed at easing the day-to-day suffering of the inmates. This included gathering food and stealing medical supplies for those most in need.

Religion was strictly prohibited in the camps. However, some Jewish women blessed lightbulbs or made Sabbath candles from hollowed-out potato peelings filled with margarine. Inmates would look out for one another while they took part in secret prayer meetings.

⬇ Inmates at Auschwitz, c.1945.

M

Think

Look carefully at the physical condition of the inmates. Why would this have made certain acts of resistance more difficult?

In 1943, one of the prisoners in the death camp at Treblinka got access to the arsenal (weapons store), from where he handed out guns and grenades to his fellow inmates. The camp was then set on fire and the arsenal exploded. In the chaos that followed, 150 prisoners escaped and 15 German guards were killed.

In the same year, Jewish inmates at Sobibor were able to kill 11 Nazis, including the camp commander, during a plan in which 300 prisoners escaped. However, the harsh winter and a hostile local population meant that most did not survive the war.

In 1944, a group of Jewish *Sonderkommandos* at Auschwitz-Birkenau managed to blow up one of the four crematoria, using dynamite smuggled in from a nearby munitions camp. Six hundred inmates escaped after the explosion, but all were killed or recaptured as they fled.

Activity

1 Looking at your completed table from Activity 1 on page 56, was the majority of Jewish resistance Active/Direct; Active/Indirect; Passive/Direct or Passive/Indirect? Explain why you think this was.

2 The Nazis did their best to portray Jews as inferior and therefore unwilling to fight back or resist. This was clearly untrue. Your task is to create a design brief for a memorial to Jewish resistance that counters this myth.

  a) Decide which type of resistance your memorial will commemorate. Will you focus on active, passive, direct or indirect examples of resistance?

  b) Include a rough sketch of what you want it to look like. Then add labels to explain your choices and a plaque summarising Jewish resistance in no more than 150 words.

6

Was the story of the twentieth century simply one of things getting better?

Was the story of the twentieth century simply one of things getting better?

Meet Irene Smith, the grandmother of one of the authors of this book. Irene was born in January 1923, which means that she was a teenager during the 1930s. She died in 2013 at the ripe old age of 90, but during the course of her life she saw many changes and lived through many of the events covered in this book. She always said that one of her favourite memories was of her husband, Ned, coming up the street in 1945 laughing and cheering because the Second World War had ended.

When Irene was born, women had only had the right to vote for five years. By the time she died the country had experienced massive changes: from the Depression of the 1930s, through the social revolution of the 1960s, to the techno music and raves of the 1990s. What aspects of life in the twentieth century do you think Irene would have found the most surprising?

As you work through this enquiry you are going to consider the degree to which various aspects of life in Britain changed over time and to develop an overview of the changes experienced by Great Britain. At the end you will be asked to consider which of the changes you think might have had the biggest impact upon Irene's life.

Britain in 1900

In 1901, 25 per cent of the working population, which numbered around 40 million, worked in the countryside. Animal power, as well as machines, was used on farms. Factories and mines regularly used steam power, and Britain led the world in heavy industry such as textiles, mining and shipbuilding. For people in need there was no unemployment benefit, nor could people claim sick pay or receive pensions.

Women were increasingly part of the workforce. This was especially true of working-class women who worked in the textiles, manufacture and service industries. However, women were generally paid less than men and could be forced out of work after the birth of a child.

People continued to work long hours but it was becoming more common to have Saturday afternoon off work. This allowed people to enjoy sporting activities and to watch cricket and football matches. The first official football club was Sheffield Wednesday, set up in 1857. Since 1871 the Bank Holiday Act had protected workers' holidays in law. By 1900 Britain boasted over 18,000 miles of railway lines, which allowed people to take breaks to beach resorts such as Brighton, Southend and Blackpool. Travel times continued to fall. By 1900 the journey from London to Edinburgh took 9 hours.

The first decade of the twentieth century saw some significant changes in education. Fewer children were expected to go out to work. By 1918 school attendance was compulsory and the school leaving age had been raised to fourteen. Education was mainly focused around securing the basics of reading, writing and arithmetic.

Activity

1 First look back at 1901 by reading the information on pages 62–63. Make a copy of the table below and add more detail to the 1900s column.
2 Then read the pages 64–69 on life for ordinary people in the 1930s, 1960s and 1990s. Record details into those columns of your table. Highlight any improvements in one colour, anything that got worse in another colour, but do not highlight examples that show no change.

Aspects of life	1900s	1930s	1960s	1990s
Work and the economy	25% worked on the land			
Health	Pensions, school medicals and unemployment insurance			
Leisure	Bank Holidays			
Politics	Programme of social reform			
Education	Compulsory schooling			

3 When your table is completed, answer the following questions.
   a) When do you think would have been the most exciting time to have been a teenager? Give reasons.
   b) Which change or changes do you think would have had the biggest impact upon Irene? Give reasons.

   Now you should be in a position to answer the big question:

   Was the story of the twentieth century simply one of things getting better?

Life expectancy for someone born in 1901 was 45 to 47 years. Thanks to the work of Louis Pasteur doctors now knew that germs were a cause of illness and vaccinations against many previously deadly diseases had been developed. Similarly, the development of anaesthetics and antiseptic had greatly increased the chances of surviving an operation. However, there was no national health service and medical care was still dependent upon having the money to pay for it.

Improvements in refrigeration had made the transportation of food more efficient. However, the poor health of recruits for the Boer Wars in 1899 and 1900 suggests that the diet of ordinary people remained limited.

The political scene in the 1900s was in a state of flux. A Liberal victory in the 1906 election saw the beginning of a programme of social reforms including pensions, school meals and insurance against sickness and unemployment. The government began to take on responsibility for the health and well-being of the people.

Protest in the 1900s often came in the form of strikes for higher pay or better conditions. The period also saw the Suffragists and Suffragettes campaign to secure votes for women (see pages 70–77).

Foreign policy was dominated by concerns for the fate of the Empire and the growing threat posed by Germany. 1914 saw Britain committing troops to the First World War following the German invasion of Belgium (see page 18).

6

Was the story of the twentieth century simply one of things getting better?

Britain in the 1930s

Affordable health care still remained out of the grasp of many ordinary working-class families. The first problem was lack of access to hospital care for anything other than tuberculosis. The second problem was the lack of access to health care for the families of working men. Many of these had no formal health cover and had to use medicines bought over the counter from the local pharmacist. As a result, an illness, needing help with a birth or calling an ambulance could cause major financial problems for families across the country.

There were improvements:

- Doctors and nurses were better trained by the 1930s.
- In 1934 local authorities started to provide school children with free milk.
- The 1936 Public Health Act encouraged local authorities to build new homes as part of a slum clearance programme, tackling damp, overcrowded and unhygienic housing.
- The 1938 Food and Drugs Act ensured that food labelling was accurate.

As a result of these changes there was a rise in life expectancy. People born in the 1930s could expect to live 'on average' to the age of 63.

Britain was still reliant on heavy manufacturing industries such as mines and shipyards. After 1929, following the **Wall Street Crash** in the USA, Britain was plunged into a period of economic depression. Between 1930–35, around 18 per cent of people were unemployed.

Hunger marches took place to highlight the problems of mass unemployment and poverty. In 1936, 200 men marched from the north east of England to London to present a petition to Parliament. This 'Jarrow Crusade' failed to secure government help, but did bring attention to the problems facing industrial working-class areas, where illness, such as tuberculosis, was rife. Britain was a divided country. In the Midlands and south east new industries such as car manufacturing and light engineering were providing work. With cheaper food, gradually rising wages and cheap mortgages, life for the growing middle classes did improve.

There were more job opportunities for women in the 1930s due to better education. Many women found work as clerks, teachers and nurses. Developments in the electronics industry allowed more women to work in manufacturing. Restrictions did remain, with many married women being prevented from working. By the end of the decade, only about ten per cent of married women were working.

⬆ The Jarrow Crusade

Throughout the 1920s the Labour Party had risen in popularity, and the Liberal Party declined; it would not form a government again in the twentieth century. The formation of coalition governments was a feature of political life in the 1930s, with the National Government (1931–40) made up of MPs from all three parties: Conservative, Liberal and Labour.

Government failure to deal with the worst aspects of the Depression encouraged the growth of extremist political parties – the British Union of Fascists led by Sir Oswald Mosley (see page 78) and the Communist Party of Great Britain. However, neither of these parties ever achieved mass support. Most of the unemployed just wanted jobs. In addition, by the early 1930s there was an earlier economic recovery than elsewhere in Europe or America. Unemployment fell, and with it earning potential improved.

British foreign policy was dominated by the growing threat of Germany. Known as the policy of appeasement, the British desperately sought an alternative to war (see page 35). The result of this was that Hitler was allowed to regain land, build up his armed forces and prepare for war, which came in 1939.

The big development in leisure for ordinary people was the rapid growth in cinema. In 1911 there had been only 94 cinemas in London. By 1930 this number had grown to 258, with a total of 344,000 seats.

While some working-class families were lucky if they were able to afford an annual trip to the seaside, there was a growing movement throughout the decade to cater for these annual trips via purpose-built Holiday Camps – such as those operated by Butlins. These offered a break away from home for working-class families while offering on-site food and entertainment.

The 1930s saw an increased interest in fresh air and outdoor exercise. Ramblers groups sprung up across the country and helped to establish the rights of ordinary people to have access to the countryside.

Education in the 1930s was split between free education and fee-paying education. The free state-funded schools were known as elementary schools, which focused on reading, writing and arithmetic, and didn't teach much else. Elementary school finished when students reached the age of 15 and most young people would go into work at that age. For the highest-achieving students, a scholarship to a fee-paying school might be possible.

Fee-paying schools had different schools for boys and girls. The most basic were the grammar schools, which were required to keep some of their places for scholarship students from the elementary schools. There also existed public schools for those who could afford the fees. Only a very small percentage of students went on to university but there were some technical colleges, which specialised in vocational subjects.

Britain in the 1960s

As the 1960s progressed, the British economy began to boom. A strong economy meant that for much of the 1960s Britain enjoyed close to full employment. Much of this economic growth and high levels of employment was built on sales of consumer goods such as washing machines and televisions, as ordinary people spent their **disposable income**. A consumer boom meant a ready supply of jobs in the manufacturing and electronics industries as well as in office work. This 'office boom' helped to ensure that there were more women in the workplace. However, with no legislation on sex discrimination, women were often treated as a source of cheap labour.

Although Prime Minister Harold Macmillan had a point when he said in 1957 'you've never had it so good', the 1960s was not all plain sailing. As the decade progressed there was growing inflation and unemployment began to rise once again.

In the field of health the 1960s was a decade of 'firsts'. The new National Health Service, established in 1948, was beginning to realise the promise of health care for all, and the advances in modern medicine were slowly being passed on to the public. Edinburgh Royal Infirmary performed the first ever British kidney transplant in 1960, while the first heart transplant took place in 1968. The mass production of contraceptive pills, the use of which rose from 50,000 to 1 million by 1961, allowed more people to plan whether or not they chose to have children. Antibiotics, better diet and an improved health service brought an increase in life expectancy. People born in 1960 could expect to live to the age of 71.

⬆ Grosvenor Square demonstration against the Vietnam War.

At the start of the 1960s British education was still split between the more exclusive 'grammar' schools and the 'secondary modern' schools. In 1965 the Labour Education Secretary began the process of creating the all-inclusive 'comprehensive' schools we know today. It represented the first step towards a comprehensive education system that served all pupils on an equal basis.

Pupils continued to receive free milk, which many disliked as it was often warm and watery. Lessons remained focused upon reading, writing and arithmetic, with neat handwriting being a desirable skill.

Another feature of education in the 1960s was the 11-plus examination, which allowed successful candidates to gain a place at grammar school. Successful graduation from grammar schools was the best route into university.

In many ways and for many teenagers, the 1960s was defined by its music. In fact the word 'teenager' had first been used on stage during a concert by Bill Hailey and the Comets in 1957. The Mersey-beat sound of the Beatles exploded onto the world stage and, by 1966, they themselves declared they were 'bigger than Jesus'. The music of the Beatles, the Rolling Stones and the Kinks was brought to a new teenage generation via 'pirate' radio stations like Radio Caroline, operating from boats in the English Channel. Access to music also came more and more through the new medium of television.

By 1960 nearly three-quarters of British households had a television. These television sets showed programmes only in black and white and provided the public with a choice of three channels.

The influence of a healthy and growing music scene in the 1960s went hand-in-hand with a growing fashion industry. Designers such as Mary Quant helped to define the decade with the classic look of the two-tone Mary Quant dress, the mini skirt and fashions inspired by the Pop Art movement of Andy Warhol.

The politics of the 1960s is often seen as quite radical. With the growth of the Campaign for Nuclear Disarmament marching in protest against nuclear weapons and protests against the American war in Vietnam, there was some truth to this idea. However, British government and indeed the British people as a whole in this period were predominantly conservative and often politics seemed out of step with the wild and crazy '**counter-culture**' image of the 1960s. There was widespread fear of mass immigration (from the Caribbean, Africa and Asia). In a speech in 1968, MP Enoch Powell warned that immigration would lead to 'rivers of blood' being spilled.

Foreign policy in the 1960s was dominated by the **Cold War**. As an ally of the United States, Britain would have been in the front line of any war against the Soviet Union. In the previous decade the government had begun a policy of spending in order to build up Britain's nuclear missile arsenal. This continued throughout the 1960s.

6

Was the story of the twentieth century simply one of things getting better?

Britain in the 1990s

The early part of the 1990s saw Britain gripped by an economic **recession**. The British economy was at its worst since the **Great Depression** of the 1930s. Unemployment began to rise and by 1991 there were 3 million British people without work. For many homeowners, the economic downturn of the early 1990s trapped them in negative equity; they suddenly found that their houses were now worth a lot less than they had paid for them.

For some ordinary British people, the late 1990s saw some improvements. One of these was due to the introduction of the minimum wage, which guaranteed that bosses had to pay workers a minimum of £3.20 per hour.

The Equal Pay Act and Sex Discrimination Act in the 1970s had meant discrimination between men and women was illegal in the workplace.

School children in the 1990s were either educated in state-funded comprehensive schools or else they attended one of the fee-paying public schools. Both types of schools offered their students a broad-based 'comprehensive' curriculum. This meant that while the old emphasis on English and maths remained, there was also the provision of sciences, humanities, languages, technology and PE. The school leaving age had risen to 16 and more students than ever, about 30 per cent of school leavers, were going on to university.

NHS Direct was set up by the National Health Service. This provided British patients with a hotline phone service, allowing them to be assessed over the telephone and directed to doctors or hospitals accordingly. The NHS also set up walk-in centres in an attempt to provide faster access to health care. In 1994 Britain's first Organ Donor Register was founded. Once again, life expectancy continued to rise. A person born in 1990 could expect on average to live to 76 years of age.

The fitness craze of the 1980s continued into the new decade. In 1992 supermodel Cindy Crawford released a fitness video that sold millions. The 1990s also saw a growing awareness of the dangers of smoking; backed by anti-smoking advertising from the government.

⬆ Poll tax riot, 31 March 1990. Police in London arrest a protester, while mounted officers look towards the crowd.

For many people in Britain, the 1990s was the start of the video game phenomenon. The Nintendo Gameboy arrived from Japan in 1990 and allowed players to sample such gaming delights as Tetris and Super Mario Bros in the palm of their hand. Mainstream music was dominated by the so-called Girl Power of the Spice Girls, the rivalry between Britpop super groups Blur and Oasis, and in nightclubs by the rapid electronic beats of techno. The dance music scene, which often featured huge raves, also led to a rise in drug use; namely the drug ecstasy. One high-profile case surrounded the death of 18-year-old student Leah Betts from complications arising from ecstasy use in 1995. On television, the 1990s introduced Britain to two US cartoon imports: *Teenage Mutant Ninja Turtles* and *The Simpsons*.

The other key electronic phenomena of the 1990s was the mobile phone. By the later 1990s the brick-like mobiles of the 1980s had been replaced by a more truly mobile phone. By 1997 phones came complete with not only a calendar and pager option but with games such as Snake.

Package holidays had been experienced by many families since the 1980s, but the 1990s saw an explosion, fuelled in large part by cheap air fares. Inter-rail passes allowed affordable travel across Europe and many students took advantage of travel opportunities in order to have a 'gap' year between school and university.

Margaret Thatcher, who had been Prime Minister since 1979, resigned on 22 November 1990. Widespread opposition to the introduction of the controversial Poll Tax had caused other members of the Conservative Party to turn against their leader. The Poll Tax required all households in Britain to pay tax based upon the number of occupants rather than upon income. Public discontent came to a head in 1990 when 200,000 protestors gathered in Trafalgar Square and the event descended into rioting. However, Thatcherism had a profound effect upon British politics. The battles of the 1980s, such as the miners' strike (see page 84) had left the unions (which protected workers' rights) greatly weakened. In addition, the closure of heavy industries such as steel, ship building and mining which followed the end of **nationalisation** signalled the end of Britain as an industrial power. The Conservatives continued under the leadership of Prime Minister John Major until the election of a Labour Government led by Tony Blair in 1997.

One achievement of the Blair government was to build upon the IRA ceasefire of 1994, leading to the signing of the Good Friday Agreement in April 1998, committing both sides to peacefully resolving the on-going problems over Northern Ireland. Outside of Ireland, and following the end of the Cold War, British foreign policy was dominated by growing concerns over the Middle East. Operation Desert Storm in 1991 saw British soldiers in action in Iraq following the Iraqi invasion of Kuwait.

Why did some women use violence to win the vote, 1901–14?

This section looks at the extension of the vote to women – the 'last step' for Britain's democracy, which you have studied growing over the past seven centuries.

The young woman in this *Daily Mirror* headline is Lilian Lenton, a 22-year-old dancer from Leicester. In February 1913, she was arrested on suspicion of having set fire to the tea house at Kew Gardens in London. She was sent to prison, where she went on hunger strike, and was force-fed. A letter to *The Times* newspaper described how 'she was tied into a chair and her head dragged backward across the back of the chair by her hair. The tube was forced through the nose twice … when the food was poured in, it caused violent choking'. What had probably happened is that the doctor had forced the tube into her lung, rather than her stomach.

It seems surprising to us that this kind of thing was happening in Britain only a hundred years ago. But Lilian Lenton was a 'Suffragette' – a member of the Women's Social and Political Union (WSPU), which had been formed in 1903 to campaign aggressively – and violently – for votes for women.

Seriously ill, Lilian was released to the home of a friend. Undaunted, she continued her campaign of **arson** – she resolved 'to burn two buildings a week … to create an absolutely impossible condition of affairs in the country, to prove it was impossible to govern without the consent of the governed'. She was arrested four more times, and went on hunger strike and was force-fed many times.

When the First World War broke out in 1914, Lilian served as a nurse in Serbia and Russia. But when she was given the right to vote, as she said later: 'Personally I didn't vote for a very long time because I hadn't either a husband or furniture.'

↑ Lilian Lenton was arrested two days before the date of this newspaper, under the pseudonym 'May Dennis', for arson to a private residence.

Think
Study Poster B.
1 What message did the artist want you to come away with?
2 How did he seek to gain the public's support for the Suffragette cause?

This picture of a forced feeding was drawn for the ➡ 1910 election by Alfred Pearse, a campaigner who drew many propaganda posters for the WSPU. Pictures like this rarely appeared on billboards or in the newspapers – they were published in Suffragette magazines or, occasionally, Suffragettes would form 'poster brigades' and walk round handing them out.

Arguing for votes for women

Book 3 of this series described the campaign for votes for women in nineteenth-century Britain, but ended by saying: 'by 1901 they had got … nowhere'.

The National Union of Women's Suffrage Societies (NUWSS) had been campaigning for votes for women since 1897. Looking at their campaign and literature, one cannot help but come to the conclusion that the 'suffragists', as they were called, were earnest but dull. By 1914 – as in 1901 – they had got 'nowhere'.

C

Votes for Mothers
THEY TELL YOU

"The Woman's Place is the Home"

Well if you had **votes** you might have **better homes**; and if you had better homes your **children** would have **a better chance**.

You have seen many a poor woman's baby as fine and healthy at birth as the child of any wealthy woman in the land. You have seen that baby gradually pine, grow thin, pale, fretful, and at last sicken and die, in spite of all its mother's love and care.

Think
Study Leaflet C.
1 What messages did the author want you to come away with?
2 How did the leaflet seek to gain the public's support for the NUWSS cause?

◆ A reconstruction of an NUWSS leaflet of July 1912.

D

Activity
1 Study page 70. In discussion with a partner or in a small group, suggest and note reasons why Lilian Lenton behaved as she did.
2 How does evidence C and D help you to understand why some young women turned to militancy?

⬆ An NUWSS rally in 1915. Look at the banner – what is its *main* message?

Campaigning against votes for women

By contrast to the NUWSS campaign, the campaign against female suffrage appears to us today to be sexist and downright stupid. Nevertheless, before the First World War, it was very successful, and even very limited 'Conciliation Bills' presented to the House of Commons in 1910, 1911 and 1912 (which would have given the vote to just one million women) failed to become law.

E

Votes for Women

While in the act of voting, Mrs Jones remembers that she has left a cake in the oven!

⬆ An anti-suffrage postcard on sale at the seaside.

Activity

3 Working in a group, suggest reasons why the campaign against women's suffrage was successful in the years 1901–14.

4 Extracts F, G and H were written by women. Suggest reasons why.

5 Working as a whole class, discuss how evidence E–J helps explain why some young women turned to militancy.

Think

1 Study Postcard E: What messages did the artist want you to come away with?

2 How did it seek to gain the public's support for the anti-suffrage cause?

F

I am satisfied with my present position, and of my almost unlimited power of usefulness, that I have no need of a vote, and should not use it if I had it.

Edith Milner, writing in *The Times*, 29 October 1906.

G

The wife of the working-man has the sole care of the children and the home; she has neither interest nor time for even rudimentary politics.

Mrs Humphry Ward, *Why I do not believe in Woman's Suffrage*, a book written in 1908.

H

The physical nature of women unfits them for direct competition with men.

Grace Saxon Mills, *Against Woman Suffrage*, a pamphlet written some time between 1910 and 1914.

I

What is the good of talking about the equality of the sexes? The first whiz of the bullet, the first boom of the cannon and where is the equality of the sexes then?

Lord Curzon, speaking in Parliament in 1912. He had been Viceroy of the British government in India, and became leader of the anti-suffrage movement, and of the campaign to preserve ancient monuments. He was aged 53 in 1912.

J

Where are the women merchants and the women bankers? Where are the women directors of great undertakings? It appears to me that it is one of the fundamental truths on which all civilisations have been built up, that it is men who have made and controlled the State.

Viscount Helmsley, speaking in Parliament in 1912. He was educated at Eton and Oxford and was aged 33 in 1912. He was killed in the First World War leading the battalion he had raised, and was buried with his favourite hunting dog.

Here come the Suffragettes!

The WSPU was formed to try to reverse the failure of the NUWSS. Led by Mrs Emmeline Pankhurst, the 'Suffragettes' adopted a much more **militant** campaign than that of the 'suffragists'. Inspired by the campaigner and cartoonist Alfred Pearse, the Suffragettes' poster campaign was modern, colourful and hard-hitting. In addition, the Suffragettes campaigned aggressively, and became steadily more violent as they:

K Shouted out in Parliament from the visitors' gallery.

Wrecked five rooms of a house MP David Lloyd George was building in Surrey through bombing it on 18 February 1913.

Disrupted political meetings by heckling the speakers.

Destroyed works of art and exhibits in galleries and museums.

Spat at and assaulted MPs.

Broke windows in public buildings and London shopping centres.

Set fire to country houses, churches, theatres and other buildings.

Poured acid, ink and tar into post-boxes to disrupt the Royal Mail.

Marched on Parliament and tried to force their way into the building.

Emily Wilding Davison ran onto the Derby racecourse and was killed on 3 June 1913 (see pages 76–77).

↑ Suffragettes waiting for the police to arrive before they chain themselves to the railings.

The Suffragettes stopped their campaign when the First World War broke out. Nevertheless, in 1918, the government gave the vote to all women over 30. In 1919, Nancy Astor became the first women to sit in Parliament. And, in 1928, all women over 21 were given the vote.

The Suffragettes were one of those rare examples in twentieth-century British history of a militant political movement.

By 2015, however, it could be argued that their efforts had been wasted. One survey found that less than one-third of young British women were interested in politics (compared to half of young men), and another found that women knew much less about political issues than men. Only 29 per cent of MPs were women, and just two-thirds of women voted in the 2015 general election.

Pages 74–77 will investigate why young women became so radically and violently involved in politics before the First World War.

Activity

6 Studying pages 70–73, list all the factors you can find which explain why some young women turned to militancy in the years 1901–14.

What motivated the Suffragettes?

Why – when most women were prepared to argue peacefully – did certain young women become so fanatically interested in politics that they became what we would today call terrorists? Historians have suggested a number of ideas:

THE SUFFRAGETTE THA

a) A great leader?

The twentieth century was the age of great leaders – did Emmeline Pankhurst inspire a generation to violence?

She certainly inspired Kitty Marion, a Suffragette arsonist, who was thrilled by 'the vigour of her intellect, the charm of her personality and above all the magnificent power of her leadership'. The WSPU London organiser, Grace Rose, even wrote a religious creed beginning: 'I believe in Emmeline Pankhurst, Founder of the WSPU'.

However, Mrs Pankhust was very difficult to work with and ran the WSPU as a dictatorship. Many supporters left or were expelled from the WSPU after quarrels with her, including her own daughter Sylvia Pankhurst.

b) Did women finally lose their temper?

The idea runs through many Suffragettes' statements that, after a century of fruitless campaigning, women finally lost patience with peaceful persuasion. Hannah Mitchell, a Suffragette campaigner, later wrote that: 'The smouldering resentment in women's hearts burst into the flame of revolt'.

c) Daring ladies?

In 1935, the historian George Dangerfield suggested that the Suffragettes were 'daring ladies' who sought adventure and suffering for 'a positively unhealthy pleasure'.

There is no doubt that many Suffragettes found their activities fun – such as Charlotte Marsh, a Suffragette activist and hunger striker 'of quiet, resolute bearing', who described breaking windows in 1912 'as though I was playing hockey'.

g) Dramatic gestures?

The historian Sheila Rowbotham (1973) suggested that Suffragettes' actions were primarily to get into the newspapers, and criticised Emmeline Pankhust for wilfully exposing her followers to danger. It is certainly true that Suffragettes often waited until the police and press had arrived before they began their actions.

NEW JIU-JITSU.

f) Working-class revolutionaries?

Mrs Pankhurst was a right-wing Tory who later admired Hitler. For many Suffragettes, however, the campaign for the vote was part of a wider bid for a social revolution. The Suffragette leader Teresa Billington-Greig was also a Trade Unionist and an organiser of the growing Labour Party, who described herself as 'a militant rebel'. Similarly, in 1914, Sylvia Pankhurst broke with her mother and went to work in the East End of London to try to bring about a social, as well as political, revolution in women's lives.

On the other hand, many other Suffragettes were middle-class women who went on the WSPU 'pilgrimages' (marches) almost as though on a picnic, wearing white dresses and hats and the WSPU colours of green and purple.

e) A collapsing society?

Britain before the First World War was a place of social unrest and trade union activism while, in Ireland, Sinn Fein and the Ulster Unionists were arming themselves for war. The First World War itself, of course, was the greatest violence of all. George Dangerfield's *The Strange Death of Liberal England* (1935) presented the Suffragettes as just one more group that refused to compromise and that used the violence as a way to overthrow the established order of things.

Were the Suffragettes, in their sphere, just a sign of the violent times?

d) Guerrillists?

Mrs Pankhurst called her activists 'guerrillists' – like modern terrorists, they sought to throw society into a continual state of fear and outrage. For many Suffragettes, this was a cool-headed decision: Mrs Bouvier (the first Suffragette to use violence when she threw stones at Home Office windows in 1909) wrote in the Suffragette magazine *Votes for Women*: 'We had decided that the time for political arguments was thoroughly exhausted, and we made up our minds that the time for militant action had arrived.'

Activity

1 In a small group, choose one of the ideas on pages 74–75, and work out ways that it would have caused certain young women to become militant Suffragettes. Consider the other ideas, and decide whether your chosen idea was more, or less, influential as a motivation to violence.
2 Debate as a whole class and put the ideas into an order of importance, from the most powerful factor to the least.

Case Study – Emily Davison

On 4 June 1913 Emily Davison, a militant Suffragette, ran out onto the race course during the Epsom Derby. She was hit by the King's horse Anmer, and died in hospital four days later.

B

⬆ A photo from one of three newsreel cameras that were recording the race at the time.

The Suffragettes immediately declared her death a **martyrdom**, and organised a huge funeral in London. Later writers, however, have not been so sure, and have suggested a number of other possibilities. Emily Davison never left any note of her intentions, so we shall never know.

Here are the facts of the case:

a) She was born in 1872 so by 1913 – at the age of 40 – she was older than most Suffragettes.

b) From 1892–95, she worked as a governess and a teacher to pay her way through an Oxford University course, gaining First-Class Honours in her exam.

c) In 1908, she became a full-time Suffragette activist. In 1912 she wrote to the Editor of *The Daily Citizen* that: 'Women had tried for years the language of reason and logic, until they realised that nothing would avail them but the language of rebellion.'

d) In the period 1908–13 she was arrested nine times; during some of these prison terms she went on hunger strike and was force-fed 49 times.

e) In 1911, on the night of the population census, she hid in a broom cupboard in the Palace of Westminster, so she could declare to the Census that her place of residence was 'in the House of Commons'.

f) In November 1912, she attacked the Reverend Jackson at Aberdeen railway station. She later claimed that she had mistaken him for the MP David Lloyd George, travelling alone and in disguise. The historian Simon Webb believes that 'no well-balanced person' would have entertained such a notion.

g) In 1912 she committed an act of arson, went to the police station, and asked to be arrested; when she was turned away, she set fire to letter boxes until she was caught. She was given six months for arson.

h) During her imprisonment in 1912, she tried a 'desperate protest … to put a stop to the hideous torture [of force feeding]… The idea in my mind was one big tragedy may save many others. When a good moment came, quite deliberately I walked upstairs and threw myself from the top, as I meant, on to the iron staircase. If I had been successful, I should undoubtedly have been killed.'

i) In 1912, in a letter to *The Newcastle Weekly Chronicle*, she wrote: 'The lessons of history teach us this, that the struggle grows fiercer and hotter towards the end, and that then is the time when every effort must be directed towards the one goal.'

j) It is sometimes suggested that she merely tried to tie a Suffragette scarf to the horse. The horse weighed half a ton and was travelling at 35mph.

k) On the day of the Derby she was helping at a Suffragette summer fair, and took the afternoon off purposefully to attend the race. Before she went she asked for two flags and, when asked why, told people to 'look in the evening paper'.

l) She had bought a return ticket to Epsom, and a family letter reveals that she intended to go to Paris after the race to care for her three-month-old nephew.

Activity

1 What motivated Emily Davison?
  ▌ A conscious martyrdom?
  ▌ A publicity stunt that went wrong?
  ▌ The action of a mad woman?

  Working as a whole class, debate your interpretation of what happened on 4 June, supporting your theories with facts from pages 76–77.

2 Looking back on your work on this section (pages 70–77), choose the five most important reasons why some young women joined the Suffragettes and turned to militancy in the years 1901–14. Use these to write an answer to the essay question:

  Why did some women use violence to win the vote, 1901–14?

  Write your essay in five paragraphs. In each paragraph:
  ▌ state your suggested reason
  ▌ develop your point with facts
  ▌ explain *why* this caused young women to become militant
  ▌ explain *how important* it was in doing so.

  Conclude your essay with a general statement of why young women turned to violence, explaining why this is your concluding opinion.

8

Was the Battle of Cable Street really a turning point in the fight against British fascism?

Was the Battle of Cable Street really a turning point in the fight against British fascism?

On a small street in London's East End, high on a wall there sits a small plaque, testament to an event about which many British people have all but forgotten.

As you learned in Section 3 about the Spanish Civil War, 1936 was an important year in the fight against European fascism. Thousands of volunteers flocked to Spain to fight against the forces of General Franco in defence of the Spanish Republic. However, the fight against fascism was not simply a European phenomenon. Fascism was on the rise in Britain, as well as on the continent. October 1936 saw the East End of London turn into a battleground between the British Union of Fascists (BUF) and an alliance of workers, Jewish residents and communists, in what became known as 'the Battle of Cable Street'.

In this section you will examine the causes and consequences of the Battle of Cable Street and evaluate some interpretations of the battle.

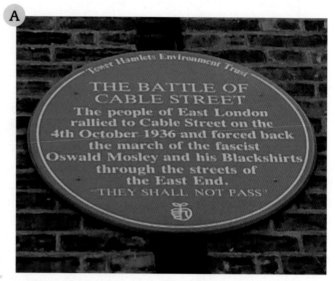

⬆ The plaque commemorating the 1936 Battle of Cable Street.

What was the Battle of Cable Street?

As you can see from the plaque in Picture A, the Battle of Cable Street was a confrontation between Oswald Mosley's British Union of Fascists (BJF), known as Blackshirts because of their uniform, and anti-fascist protestors. Mosley was inspired by the fascist one-party state of Mussolini's Italy (see page 30).

Mosley wanted to demonstrate the strength of the BUF by marching thousands of uniformed fascists through the East End, which at the time contained a large Jewish population. For their part, the anti-fascists mobilised themselves to stand in the way of the BUF. These anti-fascists, variously estimated as numbering between 100,000–250,000, consisted of ordinary working-class residents, and members of the local Jewish and Irish community, as well as Communists, Socialists and **Anarchists** who had travelled to the area for the showdown.

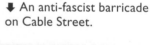

⬇ An anti-fascist barricade on Cable Street.

The result of this showdown was a day of running battles between anti-fascists and the Metropolitan Police, who had been deployed onto the streets to guard the marching route of the BUF.

Some of the action from the Battle of Cable Street can be seen in Picture B.

C

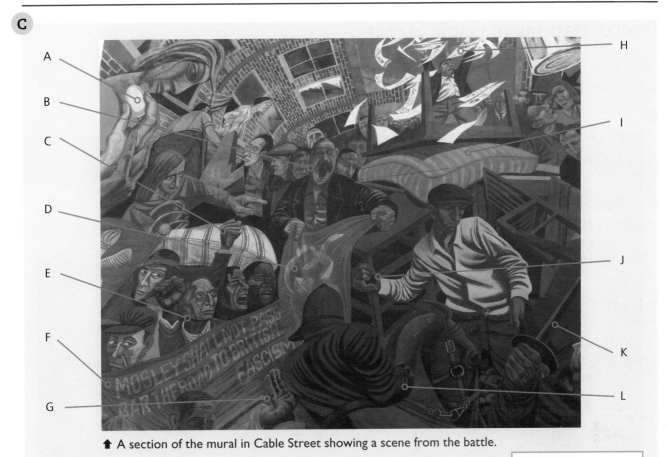

A
B
C
D
E
F
G
H
I
J
K
L

⬆ A section of the mural in Cable Street showing a scene from the battle.

As you can see in Picture B, the anti-fascists had built barricades to block the fascists' marching route. When the police tried to clear these obstacles, violence erupted. The protestors armed themselves with makeshift weapons such as chair legs and bricks and fought with the police for most of the day. A total of 150 people were arrested, and 175 injured. Mosley was persuaded that it was too dangerous to continue with the march and the fascists were herded out of the East End.

The anti-fascists proclaimed Cable Street a victory over fascism, and it led to the passing of the 1936 Public Order Act. This act made it illegal to wear political uniforms in public. Effectively, the British Union of Fascists was never allowed to march in uniform again.

Think

Look at Picture C. What labels would you add to replace each of the letters? (Suggested answers on page 139.)

Activity

I At the end of this enquiry you will be asked to make a judgement on whether the Battle of Cable Street was a turning point in the fight against fascism in Britain. At this point in the enquiry, where would you place yourself on the spectrum of opinion below? Explain why you made that choice.

Cable Street
defeated the BUF

Cable Street helped
to weaken the BUF

The BUF got stronger
after Cable Street

8

Was the Battle of Cable Street really a turning point in the fight against British fascism?

Interpretations of Cable Street

In the years since 1936, various attempts have been made to offer interpretations of the importance of this event. One such interpretation is the mural on Cable Street. Another section is shown below.

D

↑ Another section of the mural from Cable Street.

Can you find:

■ thowing milk bottles
■ a jerry pot of urine thrown over the fascists
■ police auto-gyro observing the actions
■ the fascists, unable to march
■ Hiltler – stripped and thrown out

Think

What is the message of the mural about the Battle of Cable Street?

As historians we know that interpretations are not always representations of exactly what happened. Another interpretation of Cable Street was offered in 1985 by English folk-punk band The Men They Couldn't Hang, in their song 'The Ghosts of Cable Street'. You can read the lyrics on page 81.

E

England, 1936.

The grip of the Sabbath day

In London town the only sound

Is a whisper in an alleyway

Men put on their gloves and boots

Have a smoke before they go

From the west there is a warning of

A wind about to blow

Like Caesar marching to the East

Marches Mosley with his men

Dressed in their clothes of deepest black

Like a gathering hurricane

This is the British Union

With its flag of black and red

A flag that casts a shadow in

Berlin and in Madrid

So listen to the sound of marching feet

And the voices of the ghosts of Cable Street

Fists and stones and batons and the gun

With courage we shall beat those blackshirts down

So mile by mile they come on down

To a place called Cable Street

And other men are waiting there

Preparations are complete

Mosley comes so close

They now can see his outstretched arm

A hand raised up that way

Never took the future in its palm

The battle broke as the fists and the batons fell

Through the barricades came the sound of the wounded yells

Jack Spot crept through with a chair leg made of lead

Brought down a crashing blow on Mosley's head

And so we learn from history generations have to fight

And those who crave for mastery

Must be faced down on sight

And if that means by words, by fists, by stones or by the gun

Remember those who stood up for

Their daughters and their sons

'The Ghosts of Cable Street' by The Men They Couldn't Hang. Jack 'Spot' Comer was a well-known local gangster.

As you can see, the overall message of the song is very similar to that presented by Mural D, namely that the anti-fascist resistance did serious damage to the British Union of Fascists. This interpretation was also supported by BBC reporter Kurt Barling on the anniversary of the battle, when he said Cable Street was a turning point. Mosley's fascists were not allowed to march in uniform again.

However, this interpretation has been queried by historian Dr Daniel Tilles, who declared that 'the battle of Cable Street still holds a proud place in anti-fascist memory, considered a decisive victory against the far right. In fact, the event boosted domestic fascism and **anti-Semitism** and made life more unpleasant for its Jewish victims'.

Activity

2 Now that you know a little more about the events of Cable Street has your opinion changed about whether the Battle of Cable Street was a turning point in the fight against fascism in Britain? Where would you now place yourself on the spectrum of opinion below? Explain why you made that choice.

3 Has your opinion changed since earlier in the enquiry? If so, explain why.

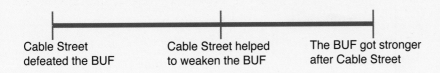

Cable Street
defeated the BUF

Cable Street helped
to weaken the BUF

The BUF got stronger
after Cable Street

Think

As you read the lyrics (E), identify the following and make two lists.

1 The parts of the song that match with your factual knowledge of the Battle of Cable Street.

2 Places where the song-writer, Paul Simmonds, has used his imagination.

8

Was the Battle of Cable Street really a turning point in the fight against British fascism?

1 **1932:** The British Union of Fascists (BUF) was formed and led by Oswald Mosley. By 1934 it had a total of 50,000 members.

4 By **1935** early signs of Britain's economic recovery from the Great Depression made Mosley's economic plans redundant. Membership of the BUF fell to 5,000.

1932

2 **1934:** The *Daily Mail*, a national newspaper with a wide readership, praised Mosley and the BUF with the headline 'Hurrah for the Blackshirts'.

3 **June 1934:** Blackshirt thugs attacked hecklers at a BUF meeting at London's Olympia – the violence damaged the BUF's reputation as it was easier to portray the party as mindless thugs.

5 **1936:** Following a shift by the BUF to a more anti-Jewish stance, attacks on Jews in the East End began to grow. This growing anti-Semitism was due to the influence of Nazi sympathisers within the party. Membership of the BUF grew by about 10,000 in this period.

⬆ Timeline: The rise and fall of the British Union of Fascists

Activity

4 Make a copy of the graph opposite. You will use it to plot the fortunes of the British Union of Fascists in the 1930s.

As you read the timeline of events, plot each one onto the graph to show the degree of success experienced by the British Union of Fascists – from a high degree of success, to a low degree of success.

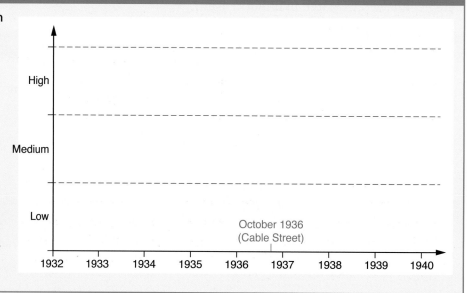

6 **4 October 1936:** Tens of thousands of anti-fascist protestors prevented 3,000 BUF Blackshirts from marching through the East End. There were running street battles centred on Cable Street.

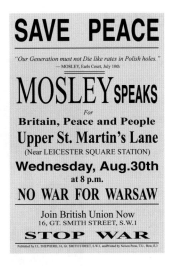

SAVE PEACE

"Our Generation must not Die like rats in Polish holes."
— MOSLEY, Earls Court, July 10th

MOSLEY SPEAKS

For

Britain, Peace and People

Upper St. Martin's Lane

(Near LEICESTER SQUARE STATION)

Wednesday, Aug.30th

at 8 p.m.

NO WAR FOR WARSAW

Join British Union Now
16, GT. SMITH STREET, S.W.1

STOP WAR

Published by J.L. SHEPHERD, 16, Gt. SMITH STREET, S.W.1, and Printed by Nelson Press, T.U., Bow, E.3

10 **1940:** With Britain at war with Nazi Germany, the BUF was declared an illegal organisation. Its meetings were banned. Mosley and 740 fascists were interned for the duration of the Second World War.

1940

7 **Mid October, 1936:** One week after Cable Street, the BUF gained 2,000 new members. Mosley made a speech to 12,000 people at Victoria Park Square in which he blamed Jews and Communists for the violence at Cable Street. According to the *Daily Mail* newspaper the speech was 'enthusiastically received'.

8 Early **1937** saw a significant increase in attacks on Jewish people and property in the East End of London. Local elections in 1937 gave the BUF its biggest ever share of the vote in the East End – it received 7,000 votes, representing an 18 per cent share.

9 **1938:** Membership of the BUF rose to 20,000 as Mosley argued that Britain should stay out of war with Germany. However, Mussolini saw the anti-Semitism of the BUF as a distraction from the real job of winning power and this saw an end to the money the BUF was receiving from Italy. Lack of funds hurt the BUF's ability to campaign effectively.

Activity

5 What does the finished graph tell you? Use it to help you answer the following questions:
   a) Was Cable Street a turning point in the fight against British fascism?
   b) What do you think was the main factor that helped to defeat the BUF?
6 After finishing the graph, has your opinion changed about whether the Battle of Cable Street was a turning point in the fight against fascism in Britain? Make a final decision where you would place yourself on the spectrum of opinion below. Explain why you made that choice.

| Cable Street defeated the BUF | Cable Street helped to weaken the BUF | The BUF got stronger after Cable Street |

7 Has your opinion changed since earlier in the enquiry? If so, explain why.
8 Write an answer to the question: Was the Battle of Cable Street really a turning point in the fight against British fascism? Make sure you use evidence to support your answer.

9

Is it possible to write an unbiased history of the Miners' Strike?

Is it possible to write an unbiased history of the Miners' Strike?

If you have seen the film or the musical *Billy Elliot*, you may not have realised that it is set against the background of real events (the Miners' Strike of 1984–85) and that its fictional town of 'Everington' is based on a real place – Easington Colliery in County Durham. In this section you will study the Miners' Strike, and assess its significance.

⬆ The cast of the Broadway musical *Billy Elliot* in Durham, North Carolina.

Background

After the Second World War, the government introduced the 'Welfare State' – a system of health, housing, education and benefits which looked after its inhabitants 'from the cradle to the grave'. Basic industries such as coal, gas, electricity and the railways were '**nationalised**' and subsidised – in 1982 the subsidy for coal was £3.05 for every ton produced.

By the 1970s, the trade unions were strong enough to negotiate aggressively with both businesses and the government. Striking became known as 'the British disease'. When the powerful National Union of Miners (NUM) went on strike in 1974, the government was defeated.

This state of affairs culminated in 'the winter of discontent' of 1978–9. Twenty-nine million working days were lost due to strike action. Inflation reached 13 per cent per annum. It seemed as though society was falling apart. As a result, the **right-wing** Tory Margaret Thatcher won the 1979 election on a platform of reducing inflation, reducing the power of the unions, and cutting tax.

Thatcher wanted to modernise British industry by exposing it to 'the chill wind' of competition … to improve or fail. Businesses reduced capacity and laid off workers. Inflation fell, but unemployment rose to more than 3 million.

In response, in 1981, the miners elected as their leader a **left-wing** activist called Arthur Scargill. He was quite open about his desire to use trade union power to topple the elected government and 'roll back the years of Thatcherism'. And so the scene was set for a clash between the NUM and the government.

The government prepared carefully for a confrontation. It stockpiled coal, and switched energy production from coal-fired to nuclear power stations. Plans were made to seize union funds, and police were trained how to handle violent **pickets**.

The Cabinet decided to provoke a strike over pit closures (which would divide the miners) rather than pay (which would unite them). On 6 March 1984, it announced the closure of 20 pits, with the loss of 20,000 jobs. Scargill claimed that the real figure was 70 pits, (although the government denied this at the time, Cabinet Papers later came to light which showed that the real figure had been 75 pits).

Immediately, large numbers of miners began walking out on strike. They were confident that they could force the government to back down.

As well as a struggle between the government and the NUM, the strike was the clash of two implacable personalities – Thatcher and Scargill.

Margaret Thatcher

A Grantham grocer's daughter who became famous as the Secretary of State for Education who stopped children's free milk at school. The Russians called her 'the Iron Lady', and the American President: 'the best man in England'.

> Let me repeat it: the losses in the coal industry are enormous. £1.3 billion last year. You have to find that money as tax-payers. It is equal to the sum we pay in salaries to all the doctors and dentists in the National Health Service.

Speaking in October 1984

> I had never had any doubt about the true aim of the Hard Left. They were revolutionaries who sought to impose a **Marxist** system on Britain, whatever the means and whatever the cost...
>
> Predictably, it was the National Union of Mineworkers, led by its Marxist president, Arthur Scargill, who were destined to provide the shock troops for the Left's attack.

Writing in 1993

Arthur Scargill

A Barnsley coalminer who joined the Young Communists aged 17 and became a Union activist. He has been called everything from 'the greatest union leader' to 'a traitor' and 'as bad as Thatcher'.

> The policies of this government are clear – to destroy the coal industry and the NUM.

Speaking in 1983

> The labour movement had the best opportunity in 50 years to transform not merely an industrial situation and win an important battle for workers in struggle, but an opportunity to change the government of the day.

Speaking in 1993

> The Tory government led by Margaret Thatcher declared war on the National Union of Mineworkers... We could either surrender right now, or stand and fight.

Writing in 2009

Activity

1 Discuss as a whole class:
- **What was at stake in the Miners' Strike of 1984–85? Make a list of issues, supporting your ideas with evidence from pages 84–85.
- **Share honestly: are you coming at this topic with an open mind, or are you already biased towards one side or the other?

9

Is it possible to write an unbiased history of the Miners' Strike?

The events of the strike

The Miners' Strike has been called 'the most bitter industrial dispute in British history'. These pages list 13 key moments of the strike:

8 MARCH 1984
The NUM called a strike. Miners in the north-east, Yorkshire, South Wales and Kent supported the strike but Leicestershire miners, and many Nottinghamshire miners, continued working.

3 MARCH 1985
The NUM conference voted by a narrow margin to end the strike.

4 NOVEMBER 1984
The Times claimed (incorrectly) that the NUM was asking for funds from the Libyan government (at the time, Libya was a country known for funding terrorists).

1 NOVEMBER 1984
MI5, who had infiltrated the NUM and was phone-tapping miners' leaders, reported that the NUM was to receive funding from the Soviet Union. Next month, an attempted $1.2m Soviet donation was blocked by a Swiss bank.

11 DECEMBER 1984
Nottinghamshire miners who had continued to work left the NUM and formed the Union of Democratic Mineworkers.

11 NOVEMBER 1984
The National Coal Board offered a £650 Christmas bonus to any miner who returned to work. After 34 weeks, many miners were forced back to work by starvation.

24 OCTOBER 1984
The NACODS union, which represented surface pit workers, had voted overwhelmingly for a strike, but called it off after doing a deal with the government about pit closures.

25 OCTOBER 1984
The High Court ordered the seizure of all NUM funds; the NUM, however, managed to move its money to Luxemburg and Eire.

11 AUGUST 1984

A rally of 23,000 working-class women marched past Downing Street; out of this grew the WAPC (Women Against Pit Closures). They organised the soup kitchens, raised money, held rallies and spoke at meetings.

3–9 APRIL 1984

Food kitchens were opened in every coalfield to feed miners' families.

21 NOVEMBER 1984

The Government reduced welfare benefits for strikers' families.

14 MARCH 1984

A court ruling instructed the NUM to stop using **flying pickets**. 8,000 police officers were sent to Nottingham.

18 JUNE 1984

There were bitter confrontations between police and the miners' pickets throughout the strike. Especially, during May, there had been trouble at the Orgreave coking plant in South Yorkshire as police tried to escort coke lorries through picket lines. This erupted into a full-scale battle on 18 June when 5,000 riot police on horseback charged 5,000 picketers; 51 picketers and 72 policemen were injured.

It seems that there are some who are out to destroy any properly elected government. They are out to bring down the framework of law … This Government will not weaken… Democracy will prevail.

Margaret Thatcher, speaking at the Conservative Conference, 12 October 1984.

We're fighting for the right to work, to save communities. Our people are suffering intolerable problems in the mining community. They haven't got food, they haven't got light, they haven't got heat. But they recognise that the only thing they can do faced with the butchery of their communities, the destruction of a way of life, is to fight.

Arthur Scargill, TV interview, August 1984.

Activity

1 Record the date and a brief description of the 13 events of the strike on pages 86–87. Arrange them in chronological order.
2 Imagine you are a Conservative supporter of the Thatcher government. Select what for you are the FIVE key events of the strike; working with a partner, explain the significance of each.
3 Repeat Task 2 as though you were a supporter of the striking miners.
4 Write two brief narrative histories of the events of the strike – the first as a supporter of the Thatcher government, the other as a supporter of the miners. Be as partisan as you like.
5 Looking at the events of the strike, can you see any reasons why it failed?
6 Share honestly with your partner: whose side, instinctively, are you on? How is it affecting the way you analyse events?

9

Is it possible to write an unbiased history of the Miners' Strike?

What was the impact of the Miners' Strike on the village of Murton?

The Miners' Strike of 1984–85 had a profound impact on communities across Britain. To get a sense of living through the strike and to assess its impact on the miners and their families, you are going to examine the recollections of two ex-miners from Murton in County Durham.

Things were quiet in Murton until 24 August 1984, when police managed to force a way for a bus carrying miners prepared to work ('scabs' to the strikers) through the picket line at nearby Easington Colliery. That night, there was a riot in Murton.

As late as 7 November, only two of the 1,600 miners at Murton Colliery had returned to work. By February, however, almost a third of Durham miners had been forced back to work, and the strikers voted to end the strike.

On 29 November 1991, Murton Colliery was closed down for ever.

⬆ Meet George and Ian. They are pictured here standing in front of the Murton Colliery Miners banner. Ian and George both still live in the village of Murton. Both men were on strike for the entire 51 weeks of the dispute.

The strike meant no wages for nearly a year; this was hard for all miners. I was luckier than some, as an electrician I had a trade and could get some work. With my mate Brian we re-wired houses, Indian restaurants, a Masonic Lodge and a bakery. All of this helped to put food on the table. Other lads with no trade other than miner did what they could. I knew men who sold flowers on the side of the motorway.

Christmas trees and turkeys were 'obtained' from farms. Lots of people faced arrest stealing coal from stockpiles at the local coking works. The miners didn't think of it as stealing; they'd dug it up in the first place. Obviously people who decided to scab (go back to work) were treated differently. The Colliery Inn, Murton's main pub, refused to ever again serve a man who broke the strike. A relative of mine, John, broke down in tears when his best mate scabbed. They never made up and the lad who scabbed left the area after the strike. I also remember an old lad called Jackie with tears on his face because he couldn't understand why he, a year from retirement, was striking to protect the jobs of young lads who were the first to break the strike.

As a working miner before the strike I was earning decent money, about £250 per week. Once the strike began, this fell to nothing. Luckily my wife had a job and my daughter had a weekend job, so she was able to give me a bit of pocket money. Also, you could get paid £2 a day for picketing, so I did as much as I could. I picketed all over the Durham coalfield.

Life did get more difficult as the strike went on. We set up a soup kitchen in the Miners' Welfare hall where anyone in the village could get a hot meal. A lot of local shops donated food to help us out. The women of the village really helped with this. There was a group called Women Against Pit Closures, they really helped to organise with collecting food and clothing as well as with running the soup kitchens. They also helped us to run a camp for the kids in the summer holidays. It gave people a break.

The strike really brought out the best in people. There was a real sense of camaraderie, of all being in this together. Murton was a very close community and people tried hard to help each other out. We also got help from overseas. The Russian miners sent bags of grain, which kept the lads who had pigeons happy. We also got lorry loads of clothes from miners in Germany. At Christmas, French miners sent us 30,000 chickens and turkeys in a refrigerated lorry. We stored them in the changing rooms of the miner's hall. It made the room so cold that the radiator pipes burst.

The longer the strike went on, the harder things got. Some men were forced back to work because they had mortgages to pay. Some men who were caught stealing coal to heat their houses were given a choice of going back to work or permanently losing their jobs. There were some, however, who went back simply because they wanted the money.

The attitude of the police was different to when I'd been on strike in the '70s. I'm not saying for a second that all of our lads on picketing duty were angels, but some of the police revelled in the violence. A lot of the police were drafted in from non-mining areas; some from as far away as London. They were highly organised with their riot shields and body armour. We got knocked about a fair bit. The first pickets arrested on the Durham coalfield were lads from Murton.

Activity

1 As you read the accounts of the two former miners, make notes of the way the strike affected life in Murton. Mark negative consequences of the strike in blue, and any evidence that it had a positive side in red. Have you got more red or blue comments?
2 Discuss as a class: Was the strike simply a disaster for the village or are there aspects of the story that can be seen in a positive light?
3 Does this side of the story – the human impact of the strike – affect your bias for or against the strike?

9

Is it possible to write an unbiased history of the Miners' Strike?

An 'End-of-Era Combat'

In April 2013, the nation marked the funeral of Margaret Thatcher. In London there was a ceremonial funeral, led by the Queen and televised on TV, with tens of thousands of mourners and admirers lining the streets (see Picture A).

In Easington in County Durham they held a party. And in the former mining village of Goldthorpe in South Yorkshire they paraded and burned an effigy in a coffin (see Picture B).

Ever since Margaret Thatcher defeated the miners, opinion about the strike has been fiercely divided. Pages 90–93 have evidence about the consequences of the defeat of the Miners' Strike of 1984–85, but you will realise that this is a subject on which no one is impartial.

> **Think**
>
> If you only had these two photographs (A and B), what could you say were the results of the defeat of the Miners' Strike?

C Economic devastation

Thatcher left a legacy of devastation across the mining communities of County Durham and the bitterness is still felt today. Mining areas like County Durham were decimated and have struggled to recover ever since.

In Easington alone, 11,000 mining jobs were lost, with a further 9,000 jobs associated with the industry.

Increased poverty, with the return of long-term unemployment, is the legacy of Margaret Thatcher's governments.

Alan Napier, Deputy Leader of Durham County Council, writing in 2015. At the time of the strike, Alan was an electrician at a mine and a Union official. Later, as a leading councillor, he had to deal with the after-effects of the strike.

D Economic renewal

When she became leader of the Conservative Party in 1975, Britain was on the brink of disaster...

Thatcher succeeded in drastically reducing inflation; taming the power of what were probably the most powerful labour unions in Europe … and establishing the conditions for long-term economic growth.

She put an end to the 'British disease'. She put Britain back to work.

An internet comment by a member of the public calling himself 'Noel's Barmy Army', May 2005.

> **Think**
>
> How do Extracts C and D differ in their assessment of Margaret Thatcher's legacy? Why?

E

The trade unions defeated

From 1982 to 1985 the conventional wisdom was that Britain could only be governed with the consent of the trade unions. No government could really resist, still less defeat, a major strike; in particular a strike by the miners' union... That day had now come and gone.

Margaret Thatcher, writing in her memoirs in 1993.

F

Women Against Pit Closures

A beautiful hand with the pastry she had

Her sponge cakes were lovely and light

But, now it's all muesli, and yoghurt, and nuts

While she's out at meetings each night

We could have gone on, for the rest of our lives

Never knowing, just what she was like

And she'd have been trapped in our image of her

If it hadn't been for the strike.

Kim, a poem by a West Yorkshire miner's mother, Jean Gittins (1985)

G

The trade unions not defeated

The miners' return to work in March 1985 did not reduce British trade unionists to a sullen [obedience] towards the Tories and the free market. A violent 51-week strike by the miners was quickly followed by a vicious 54-week disruption by print workers.

Graham Stewart, *Bang! A History of Britain in the 1980s*, 2013.

H

I

Pit closures – facts

For the miners themselves the impact of the strike's defeat has been devastating. There were 170 pits in the UK when the strike began, employing over 181,000 men. Today, there are 15 pits employing around 6,500 men.*

Areas once defined by their connection with mining such as Durham and Lancashire now have no pits.

Chris Marsden and Julie Hyland, *Britain: 20 years since the year-long miners' strike*, 2004.

* In 2015 the last three deep-level mines in the UK were closed.

J

Pit closures – effects

Soon after, the government's program of 'accelerated closure' was put into practise.... With no regard for the devastation this would wreak upon British mining communities, Thatcher continued her plan in the name of the privileged minority. The majority [were] left with unemployment, poverty and no chance for a happy or peaceful existence.

'Notes on the Miners' Strike' – an internet article, written in 2007 by someone called 'Steven'.

9

Is it possible to write an unbiased history of the Miners' Strike?

K Results of the strike

The strike cost 26 million days' work lost to the National Coal Board and a massive fall in production. Britain lost 1.2% of growth in 1984 because of the strike.

The miners were totally demoralised after the strike... The 'miners' culture' had been destroyed. The miners were now aware that there was no future left in the coal industry, and they often preferred to take the money they were offered to leave the industry...

The Thatcher years did not in the short run lead to any significant improvement in the British economic position. But in the medium term ... Britain did in fact enjoy a genuine economic revolution during the 1980s. The prosperity of the British financial industry reached proportions unknown in modern history. The financial industry contributed to the establishment of a class of newly wealthy people, the 'yuppies'.

The French economist PF Gouiffès, *Thirteen Years That Changed Britain*, 2009.

L The cost of the strike

We are where we are today because the miners and their allies lost a battle we were forced to fight. Thirty years ago Britain was awash with energy – coal, gas, and North Sea oil – but now we are in the midst of an energy crisis...

The total cost of the strike, the decimation of communities, loss of earnings, the switch to inefficient and more expensive fuels, social security payments, policing, ill health, etc., are ongoing, and rising, and likely to reach £100 billion.

Where we are today, as a country, shows the importance, and significance, of the miners' fight.

David Douglass, writing in the *ASLEF* [a trade union] *Journal*, February 2014.

> **Think**
>
> Pierre-François Gouiffès (Extract K) is French. Might this have helped him be objective in his comments on the strike?

M A sea-change in politics

The Miners' Strike became the defining event of British politics in the 1980s. And in retrospect, it's clear that it was the last class-focused dispute of its kind... Many of the political battles of the past two decades have actually been battles over cultural values, be it marriage, family, sexuality, abortion, immigration, multiculturalism, Islam or the EU.

The trade unions of today are caricatures of their pre-1985 predecessors. They rarely fight. Instead, they prefer to offer a variety of consumer services to their members – insurance, holidays, legal assistance in tribunals, and so on.

Frank Furedi, 'sociologist and commentator', in an internet blog, 2015.

N A necessary shock

After the necessary shock treatment of the early '80s the UK had 20 years of unparalleled economic growth.

Internet comment by a member of the public calling himself 'JoeDM', 2015.

O A disaster

A defeat for the whole working class, a defeat for us all.

Terry Thomas, NUM vice-president in South Wales during the strike, speaking in 2014.

Defeat

"JUST WAIT TILL NEXT TIME!"

⬆ A cartoon by the cartoonist Stanley Franklin, published 4 March 1985 in *The Sun* newspaper. (*The Sun* was a right-wing paper which opposed the strike.)

Activity

1 Using Evidence E to P (pages 91–93), choose the TEN most important results which the different writers have suggested were consequences of the strike; write them on ten cards:
  ▌ Divide them into 'positive' and 'negative' perceptions.
  ▌ Divide these again into 'short-term' and 'longer-term' results.
2 Being as impartial as you can, write an objective account of 100 words on '**The Impact of the Miners' Strike of 1984–85**'.
3 Allowing your personal beliefs and feelings free rein, write 100 words on what you really feel about '**The Impact of the Miners' Strike of 1984–85**'.
4 Discuss as a class: Is it possible to write an unbiased history of the Miners' Strike?

Think

1 Study Cartoon P and make a list of the significant elements of the scene.
2 Use your list to explain the message of the cartoon.

93

The decline of the British Empire in the twentieth century

In 1918, as a result of the various treaties following Britain's victory in the First World War, the biggest empire the world had ever seen grew even larger.

However, in 1947, the largest and most important possession in the empire, India, became independent. By the end of the 1960s, the majority of Britain's other colonies had gone the same way. Today, virtually all of the countries once under British control are independent. In this section (pages 94–105) you will explore the reasons why the British Empire declined so rapidly.

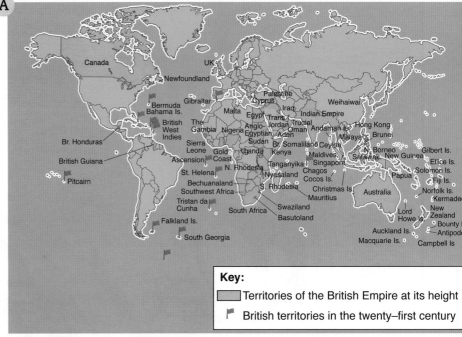

A

Key:

- Territories of the British Empire at its height
- 🚩 British territories in the twenty–first century

⬆ Map of the British Empire at its height in 1920. The flags show all that remains of the Empire today.

A celebration of independence

In the summer of 2014, David Wright left his home near Solihull and took a plane to Zambia in southern central Africa. Zambia, previously called Northern Rhodesia, had been part of the British Empire since 1889. David had been invited by the Zambian government to join the celebrations for the fiftieth anniversary of the country's independence.

Between 1958 and 1968, David was a District Officer looking after an area with a population of 10,000 people. His many responsibilities included maintaining law and order, developing local government, improving farming methods, tax collection and repairing local roads – enough to keep anyone busy!

Jumped or pushed?

It is clear that in 1964, the British government fully supported independence in Zambia. Officials like David Wright stayed on to ensure the smooth running of the newly independent state. It seemed that the British were willing to give up parts of the Empire. Just four years earlier, the British Prime Minister had signalled as much in a speech (see Extract C, page 95).

B

⬆ David Wright and Kenneth Kaunda, Zambia's first leader after independence, 1968.

C

...the most striking of all the impressions that I have formed since I left London a month ago is of the strength of this African national consciousness. In different places it takes different forms, but it is happening everywhere. The wind of change is blowing through this continent and whether we like it or not, this growth of national consciousness is a political fact. And we must all accept it as a fact, and our national policies must take account of it.

The famous 'wind of change' speech by the British Prime Minister, Harold Macmillan.

Think

What words did Macmillan use Extract C to make African independence sound widespread and unstoppable?

D

In Northern Rhodesia, the British handover of power to the new independent Zambia under President Kaunda was speedy and smooth. I helped train the new administration before and after independence.

David Wright in 2015, recalling his time in Zambia 1958–68.

The big question running through this section asks whether the British Empire 'jumped' (granted independence willingly to its colonies) or was 'pushed' (forced to give up the colonies). It is clear from David's comments and experiences in Zambia that he believes the British 'jumped'. In the rest of the section you will look at a range of colonies and weigh up the reasons why they became independent.

After empire

Today, most of Britain's former colonies make up the Commonwealth of Nations. The Commonwealth Games are the third-largest multi-sport event in the world. They are called the 'Friendly Games' and pride themselves on bringing together nations with the shared values of democracy, human rights and the rule of law.

E

The special strength of the Commonwealth lies in the combination of our diversity and our shared inheritance in language, culture and the rule of law; and bound together by shared history and tradition; by respect for all states and peoples; by shared values and principles and by concern for the vulnerable.

Extract from the *Commonwealth Charter*, 2013.

Activity

1. What does the continued existence of the Commonwealth suggest about the way the British Empire ended? Does it give you any clues as to whether the British 'jumped' or were 'pushed'?
2. Based on what you have learnt about the history of the twentieth century so far, can you think of any events or changes that might have forced Britain to give up its empire?
3. Should we, as historians, simply rely on the experiences of David Wright and his time in Zambia? Give your reasons.

Had the British lost the right to govern in 1947?

In 1900, India was the most prized possession of the British Empire – its 'jewel in the crown'. 300 million people lived under the British Raj (British rule) in an area that covered the present-day countries of India, Pakistan, Burma and Bangladesh. Many British officials saw their mission in India as preparation for 'one day' handing the country back to the Indians. However, to most British in India, that day seemed a very long way off. Yet, in 1947, this treasured part of the empire was declared independent. In this chapter you will investigate why this happened and also consider whether the British 'jumped' or were 'pushed' out of India.

How the British justified the Raj

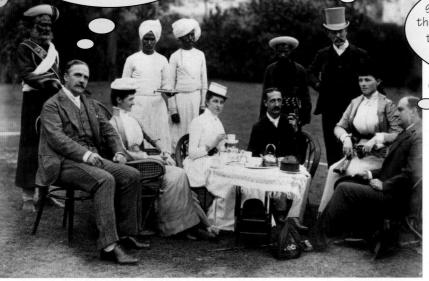

Our presence here keeps the country safe from outside aggression. We protect India from attack by other countries with our powerful army and navy.

The British are the glue holding this diverse country together. There are over a thousand languages spoken and deep religious divides. Two-thirds of Indians are Hindus. Most of the rest are Muslims, but there are also Sikhs, Buddhists, Christians and a number of other faiths.

We ensure good government in India, and look after the interests of all Indians. Moreover, the Empire is a global marketplace which helps the British and the Indians to benefit.

A
← A British tea party in India, c.1900. The British liked to argue that the Raj was there to help India. They made several arguments to justify British rule.

British rule in India

The British built a railway system to link the country and laws were enforced by British magistrates. English became the official language and was the only way that some Indians, who spoke many different languages, could talk to one another.

Some historians argue that the Indian economy was run in a way that helped Britain rather than the native population. India supplied the raw materials, such as cotton, that Britain used to produce goods. Very little Indian industry was developed in case it began to compete with British manufacture.

By the 1920s and 1930s, the British were employing large numbers of Indians in the administration of the country. However, the most important jobs in the army and civil service were always given to the British.

There were some rich Indians who sent their sons to schools in England. They learnt about democracy and saw that people in Britain enjoyed freedoms that most Indians could only dream of. A number of future leaders in the independence movement were educated in England.

The First World War

During the First World War (pages 11–27), Britain needed all of the soldiers it could get. Despite the conflict having almost nothing to do with them, over 1 million Indian soldiers fought for the British. In return, the British promised India more self-government.

B

← Indian soldiers on the Western Front during the First World War.

Think

Indian troops risked their lives and came into contact with soldiers from France, Britain and the USA. How might this have influenced their thinking when they returned home?

In 1919, the British government passed the Government of India Act. Indians were given powers to deal with health, agriculture and education. However, all decisions could be blocked by the Viceroy (the British governor of India) and the British kept control of finance and the law. Many Indians were bitterly disappointed and there were widespread protests.

Things came to a head later that year at Amritsar, where the British ordered troops to fire on a demonstration of 5,000 Indians. Around 1,000 Indians were injured and nearly 400 were killed. Following Amritsar, Gandhi (see page 98) argued that, 'When a government takes up arms against its unarmed subjects, then it has lost the right to govern.'

Activity

1 The British believed that their rule over India was completely justified. Discuss, based on your research so far, if Gandhi was right that British rule was no longer justified following Amritsar.

2 Copy the chart below. Use the information on pages 96–97 to help decide whether British actions lived up to their justifications for ruling India. Wait until your chart is complete after the activity on page 99 before making a final decision about the scores.

Justification for the Raj	Score 1–10	British actions
The British were the glue holding the diverse country together.		
The British protected India from outside aggression.		
The British ensured good government that benefited all Indians.		

Gandhi

Throughout the 1920s and 1930s, one man above all others came to represent the campaign for Indian independence. His name was Gandhi and he turned demands for Indian independence into a mass movement.

a) Born in 1869, Gandhi spent time in Britain training as a lawyer before moving to South Africa. In 1915, he returned to India to help in the independence movement.

C

g) Other protests followed the Salt March, and the British responded with 20,000 arrests. Some prisoners were flogged. However, in 1931 and 1932 Gandhi was invited to London. A new Government of India Act was passed in 1935 giving more powers to Indians, but still far short of independence.

f) In 1930, Gandhi and his followers went on a 380-km march to the coast to make salt. Salt production was controlled by the British who made a fortune selling it to the Indians.

e) Gandhi argued independence would help to end poverty and suffering in India. He urged Hindus and Muslims to work together to achieve this.

b) Gandhi lived a strict life. He was a vegetarian, often fasted, wore only a loin cloth and abstained from sex. His core belief was that truth and right would always triumph in the end.

c) Gandhi believed in non-violent protest. He encouraged the use of strikes, marches, sit-down protests and boycotts. Even when attacked, his followers would not fight back.

d) Gandhi made a point of spinning his own cotton every day. This helped encourage a boycott against buying British-made cotton clothing that could be produced in India.

⬆ Mohandas Gandhi spinning cotton, c.1930.

The Second World War

Once again Indian soldiers fought and sometimes died for the British. In 1942, the Japanese army swept aside British forces in Asia and occupied India's neighbour Burma. Suddenly, it appeared the British might not be able to protect India. Some Indians, encouraged by Japanese propaganda (see Poster D), switched sides and joined the Indian National Army to fight the British.

↑ Japanese propaganda poster aimed at Indians, c.1942.

By 1943, food shortages in Bengal became a famine. The British had not introduced **rationing** to make supplies go further and had failed to distribute food to the neediest areas. Between 3 and 4 million Indians had died from hunger and disease by 1944.

Independence

In 1945, Britain had a new Prime Minister, Clement Attlee. He was committed to the idea of Indian independence. However, Muslims were worried that the Hindus would dominate an independent India. In 1946, fearing India was slipping towards civil war, Attlee appointed Earl Mountbatten as Viceroy. He rushed through reforms to try and avoid further bloodshed. In August 1947, the independent states of India and Pakistan were created. Around 400,000 people had died in the violence by the time the British pulled out.

> **Think**
>
> Many Indians could not read, so how do the images in Poster D get its message across?

E

Is it any wonder that today she [India] claims – as a nation of 400,000,000 people that has twice sent her sons to die for freedom – that she should herself have freedom to decide her own destiny? My colleagues are going to India with the intention of using their utmost endeavours to help her to attain that freedom as speedily and fully as possible.

Speech by British Prime Minister Clement Attlee, 1946.

> **Think**
>
> Is Attlee's speech (Extract E) evidence that the British 'jumped' or were 'pushed' out of India?

Activity

3 Using the information on pages 98–9, add more detail to the chart you started in Activity 2 on page 97. Once you have completed your chart you can decide on scores and fill in the second column.

4 Discuss as a class whether Britain had lost the right to govern by 1947. Be prepared to explain your thinking.

5 Next, you are going to focus on the big question in this section: whether the British Empire 'jumped' or was 'pushed'. Make your own copy of the chart below and use the information on pages 96–99 to help you fill it in.

Evidence suggesting the British 'jumped' out of INDIA	Evidence suggesting the British were 'pushed' out of INDIA

Why did Britain hang on to Malaya for so long?

We have already seen that following the Second World War, Britain seemed in a quite a hurry to withdraw from India (see pages 98–9). By 1954, the British were the only remaining colonial power left in south-east Asia. Yet they continued to hold on to Malaya until 1957, despite having withdrawn from India ten years earlier. In this chapter you will use the comic strip to investigate the reasons why the British hung on for so long.

A

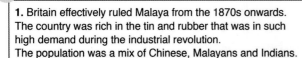

1. Britain effectively ruled Malaya from the 1870s onwards. The country was rich in the tin and rubber that was in such high demand during the industrial revolution.
The population was a mix of Chinese, Malayans and Indians.

2. During the Second World War, the Japanese occupied Malaya from 1942 to 1945. The Malayan Peoples' Anti-Japanese Army (MPAJA) led the resistance. The MPAJA disarmed when the British promised to grant equal rights to the Chinese community and greater independence.

3. After the war, Britain was in huge debt to the USA. Malayan rubber and tin exports were a good way for Britain to earn the dollars needed to pay America back. Britain began to strengthen its control over Malaya and step up production.

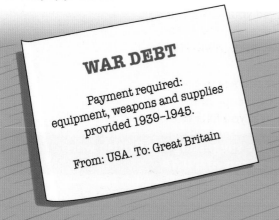

WAR DEBT

Payment required: equipment, weapons and supplies provided 1939–1945.

From: USA. To: Great Britain

4. In 1948, the communist-controlled Malayan National Liberation Army (MNLA) began a guerrilla war against the British. The MNLA targeted tin and rubber production, attacking workers and carrying out acts of sabotage.

5. The USA was usually against empires, but was also concerned about the spread of communism. China had become communist, and the Americans feared other countries might follow. Therefore, they supported British rule as a way of preventing this.

Hmm, end imperial rule or stop communism?

6. The British banned the Communist Party and gave the police powers to arrest and lock up people without trial. They sent around 35,000 troops to crush the MNLA; 500,000 Chinese Malayans were forced into villages surrounded by barbed wire to prevent them supporting the MNLA.

7. Between 1950 and 1953, the USA went to war in Korea. The need for military vehicles increased demand for natural rubber. The British made a fortune from rubber sales and used the money to fight the communists and win more support from the Malayan public through improved health care and propaganda.

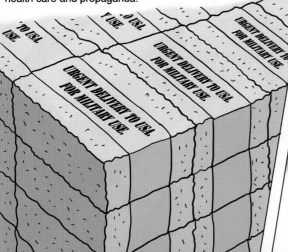

COMMISSIONER OF WORKS

8. By 1952, the British realised the need to speed up political change. Increasing numbers of Malayans were appointed to government posts. In 1954 the British government promised independence once the communists were under control. This effectively ended Malayan support for the communists and, in 1957, Malaya became independent.

Activity

1 Make a list of the possible reasons why the British were so slow to leave Malaya. Which of these do you think was the most important?

2 Did the Korean War help speed up or slow down the move towards independence? Explain your answer.

3 Next, you are going to focus on the big question in this section: whether the British Empire 'jumped' or was 'pushed'. Make your own copy of the chart below and use the information on pages 100–101 to help you fill it in.

Evidence suggesting that the British 'jumped' out of Malaya	Evidence suggesting the British were 'pushed' out of Malaya

Why did Kenya become so violent on its journey to independence?

By 1900, Africa had been divided up between the European powers. The British government believed they could bring better laws, religion, roads, railways, medicine and farming methods to their colonies. Kenya became independent in 1963, in the same decade as most of Britain's other African colonies.

However, Kenya experienced a lengthy period of violence in which hundreds of Africans were killed. The Mau Mau uprising (1952–60) was in total contrast to the experiences of other British African colonies like Zambia (see pages 94–95), where the path to independence had been much more peaceful. On pages 102–103 you will investigate why Kenya became so violent.

d) Black Africans living in Kenya were forced to live in overcrowded tribal reserves. They were prohibited from growing certain valuable crops. Only white settlers could grow coffee. This ensured prices stayed high, bringing them more profit.

A

c) In most British colonies, the Africans were governed by 'indirect rule'. The existing chiefs ruled, but under the supervision of a British 'adviser'. This kept land in the hands of the Africans even if it was only a few. In Kenya there was no indirect rule and white settlers dominated the council that ran the country. The whites had total control over the land.

b) After the First World War, the British government helped white army officers move to Kenya. Around 3,000 whites controlled 12,000 miles of the best land, known as the 'White Highlands' as no Africans were allowed to farm there. Only Southern Rhodesia and Kenya had a large white population. Ghana, Nigeria, Uganda, Northern Rhodesia and Nyasaland had only small numbers of white settlers living there.

a) The British believed in the idea of 'trusteeship', meaning that one day the Africans would be allowed to rule themselves. However, there was little agreement about how far into the future this would be.

⬆ Suspected Mau Mau rebels in a British detention camp, 1954. In 2013, the British government apologised and promised compensation to hundreds of Kenyan men who had been imprisoned, beaten and even tortured in the camps.

Activity

1   Make your own large copy of this Venn diagram. Use the information in the boxes on pages 102–103 to fill in the diagram and show the differences between Kenya and Britain's other African colonies.

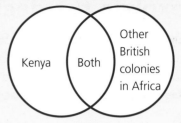

2   Use your completed diagram to decide what made Kenya so violent in the 1950s. Think about the following things:

   a) What disadvantages faced black Africans living in Kenya compared to those in other British colonies?

   b) What were the main reasons for these disadvantages?

3   Next, you are going to return to the big question in this section, whether the British Empire 'jumped' or was 'pushed'. Make your own copy of the chart below and use the information on pages 102–103 to help you fill it in.

Evidence suggesting that the British 'jumped' out of Kenya	Evidence suggesting the British were 'pushed' out of Kenya

4   Now that you have studied what happened in India, Malaya and Kenya, you should have your own view on the section question: **Did the British Empire 'jump' or was it 'pushed'?** Be prepared to back up your argument with facts and opinions.

e) At the outbreak of the Second World War in 1939, 90 per cent of Kikuyu tribesmen from Kenya were rejected on health grounds from joining the army. This was mainly due to malnutrition.

f) Thousands of black African troops served in the armed forces during the Second World War. Many came into contact with soldiers from other parts of the Empire and this opened their eyes to new ways of thinking.

g) After 1945, Britain hoped to solve its economic problems at home by making more money from its African colonies. Britain sent agricultural experts to improve farming methods and this aroused suspicion and resentment.

h) Many Africans, including Kenyans, were inspired by the success of the independence movement in India. They saw what was possible and felt encouraged to ask for greater freedoms.

i) Britain had justified having African colonies as bases from which it could protect trade routes to India. After 1947, these were no longer needed.

k) The Mau Mau uprising led British authorities to make changes to avoid further bloodshed. In 1957, the first elections for black Kenyans were held and in the following year there were the same number of blacks as whites on the ruling council. Crop restrictions were lifted, which meant black Kenyans could grow whatever they wanted. In 1959, the 'White Highlands' were opened to Africans and by 1963 Kenya was independent.

j) White settlers in Kenya put pressure on the British government to outlaw any kind of protest movement. This forced nationalist groups to go underground, making them more radical and desperate. When the Mau Mau uprising broke out in 1952 it led to terrible violence.

'Vast, variegated and far flung.' How should we explain the decline of the British Empire?

So far in this section (pages 94–103) you have looked at a range of case studies about the decline of Britain's Empire. You have made judgements about how far Britain 'jumped' or was 'pushed' out of India, Malaya and Kenya. But was it really that simple?

 A

It is perhaps obvious that no simple or single cause will be sufficient to account for the break-up of such a vast, **variegated** and far flung empire as the British.

Historian, John Darwin, 1991.

The historical debate

Broadly speaking, historians use three important factors to help explain the end of the British Empire. These are explained in Illustration B below. These go beyond the simple idea of being 'pushed' or choosing to 'jump'. They also argue that these factors often linked together to bring about change.

Think

Can you think of ways that these three factors (B) might have linked together?

B

1 Various British governments took the decision to give up the empire. Over time the colonies had less economic and military value and were costing more to protect. The British public gradually lost their appetite for empire.

2 Nationalists living under British control fought for independence and this put the British government under pressure to grant it.

3 The Second World War changed the world, which after 1945 was dominated by the 'superpowers'. The Soviet Union and USA disapproved of the empire for different reasons. Britain was too weak to remain a world power and was 'squeezed out'.

Activity

1 The statements below give you some further facts about the decline of the British Empire to add to the information you found out on pages 96–104. Which of the three factors in Illustration B (page 104) might they be used to support? Be careful, some of the statements might support more than one factor.

a) The cost of protecting the empire was very high. After 1945, the main threat to Britain came from the Soviet Union. Britain needed to spend money on deploying troops in Europe to counter this.

b) In 1956, when Britain sent troops to capture the Suez Canal in Egypt, the international community, including the USA, was outraged. Britain was humiliated and forced to back down.

c) After the Second World War, Britain was in massive debt to the USA. The country was also heavily dependent on American aid.

d) Violence in Ireland had forced the British to **partition** the country in the 1920s. This sent a message to other parts of the empire that armed uprisings could bring results.

e) Having fought against Nazi Germany in the Second World War, the British people were more interested in freedom than in using force to control people.

f) A good number of nationalist leaders were given training and studied in the Soviet Union. They went back to their countries full of new ideas about the unfairness of empires and demands for greater equality. Many thought communism was the answer.

g) Troops from the empire, especially India, had fought for Britain in both world wars. Many wanted more freedoms in return.

2 You have looked at a range of different countries and found out more about the historical debate surrounding the decline of Britain's empire. Now it is time to answer the big question:

Did the British Empire 'jump' or was it 'pushed'?

The framework below will help you to structure your answer.

Paragraph 1 – introduce the question and explain to the reader what is meant by 'jumped' and 'pushed'. You could make this more interesting by including the story of David Wright and the impression that he gives about how the British left Africa willingly (jumped). Use pages 94–95 to help you.

Paragraph 2 – set out the evidence that supports the idea that the British 'jumped' and willingly gave up their empire. Use the pushed/jumped charts you completed and the information on pages 99–103 to help you.

Paragraph 3 – set out evidence that supports the other side of the argument, that the British were 'pushed' out of their empire. Use the pushed/jumped charts you completed and the information on pages 99–103 to help you.

Paragraph 4 – make a judgement and spell out what you think is the answer to the big question. Really good conclusions will refer to the historical debate and the supporting statements on pages 104–105 to help explain the decline of Britain's empire.

What is the story of Germany from 1933 to 2015?

Between 1945 and 1990 Germany was two countries, not one. It had a Western half that was capitalist (the Federal Republic of Germany or BRD) and an Eastern half that was communist (the German Democratic Republic or DDR). This section looks at how the history of East Germany has been interpreted.

There are many different forms of interpretation:

- academic texts, where historians present a specific argument
- works of fiction, like novels or films
- those with an educational purpose, like museums or textbooks.

In this section (pages 106–119) you will have an opportunity to analyse these different types of interpretation.

Before you do that, you need some background knowledge. Pages 106–107 introduce the story of Germany from 1933 to 2015. It is important you understand this to be able to analyse the different interpretations in the rest of this section.

1933–45 – Nazi Germany
In these years the country was ruled by Hitler and the Nazi Party as a dictatorship, where large numbers of people were persecuted and murdered. The people lived in fear and were strictly controlled. The Nazis began the Second World War (see pages 34 to 45), which ravaged Germany.

1950s – Mass emigration
The capitalist Western half of Germany prospered, whereas the communist-run Eastern half did not. There were better-paid jobs and a wider range of food and items to buy in the West. As a result, many East Germans moved to the West. Although the borders between the countries were closed, large numbers poured through the open Berlin borders and flew out of West Berlin. By 1961 3.5 million East Germans had left; approximately 20 per cent of the entire East German population.

YOU ARE LEAVING THE AMERICAN SECTOR

1933 1935   1940   1945   1950   1955   1960

1945 – Allies invade
In 1945 the **Allies** invaded Germany and defeated the Nazis. The British, Americans and French invading from the West took control of that half. The Soviets invading from the East took control of the rest. All four Allies shared control of Berlin. Borders between the two halves of the country were closed except for the border in Berlin, which all four agreed would stay open so that the city could continue to operate.

Activity

1 Summarise the history of Germany into less than 50 words. Compare your summary with those of three other people in your class. Was your interpretation the same as theirs?
2 At the end of this section (page 118) you are going to be asked to create a museum about East Germany. You can start this now. If you were opening an exhibition on the history of East Germany, what title would you give it? (Make it short and snappy!)

1989 – The fall of the Wall
In 1989 protests against the communist East German government began in the town of Leipzig. By November the protests had spread to Berlin and over half a million people were on the streets. On 9 November the government bowed to pressure and decided to open all the borders. Thousands gathered at the checkpoints and were released. East and West met and embraced. Demolition of the Wall began that evening by the hands of the people.

1961 – The Berlin Wall
By 1961 the East German government needed to do something to stop the emigration. With the backing of the Soviet Union, they built a wall which encircled the entirety of West Berlin. The Wall cut streets in half and meant that some people would not see their families again for 28 years. The Wall left West Berlin an isolated island in the middle of a communist country.

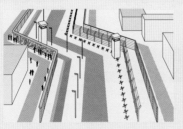

| 1965 | 1970 | 1975 | 1980 | 1985 | 1990 |

1961 to 1989 – A tale of two Germanys
For 28 years the two different Germanys continued down very different paths. The capitalist Western half grew economically and under a democracy the people experienced freedom. The communist Eastern half struggled to grow economically and the people were strictly controlled by the dictatorship of the Socialist Unity Party.

1990 onwards – Unification
In March 1990 the first free elections were held in East Germany and the communists were defeated. The new coalition of non-communist parties in East Germany actively sought reunification with West Germany. In October the two countries became one again. This led to large changes for some, especially the East Germans, but today Germany has emerged as one of the strongest countries in Europe.

How and why have interpretations of life in East Germany changed so much in the last fifty years?

Interpretations of life in East Germany are very different and have changed a lot over the last fifty years. Your challenge is to work out why.

East Germany is a vile dictatorship.

1980

I miss East Germany. It was a lovely time to live.

1995

It's more complex than this, it was 'the people's **paradox**'

2005

Enquiry step 1: First evidence – asking questions

Have a look at three characters above. What questions do they make you want to ask about East Germany?

To answer the enquiry question we need to know three things:

- First, what are the details of each interpretation?
- Second, whose point of view do the interpretations represent?
- Third, why did these particular interpretations come about when they did?

The traditional interpretation – East Germany the dictatorship?

The first interpretation of East Germany that we are going to examine was dominant from the erection of the wall in 1961 to its fall in 1989. It focused on **oppression**, with many in the West saying that this was Germany's 'second dictatorship' (with Hitler's being the first dictatorship).

Enquiry step 2: Suggesting an answer

1 In the table below are four criteria to judge a dictatorship. Read the information about East Germany on pages 109 to 110 and then make a judgement about the extent it was a dictatorship in each criteria.

	To what extent was East Germany a dictatorship? Give it a rating out of 10	Explain why you gave it this rating
Rule by a single party		
Total control over means of communication		
Control of the economy		
Police using terror as a control tactic		

2 In pairs discuss and suggest a reason why this interpretation of East Germany as a dictatorship would be dominant in the West in the 1980s. CLUE: Look back at the timeline of the story of Germany on pages 106–107 and think about the political situation.

3 Suggest an initial answer to the question **How and why have interpretations of life in East Germany changed so much in the last fifty years?**

A

Rule by a single party

East Germany was run by the Socialist Unity Party of Germany (SED) from 1946 to 1990. The country was governed by a National Front coalition of parties, but all of these were controlled by the SED. Party leaders and senior officials were given special treatment with better cars, better homes and better shops. An uprising in protest against the SED in 1953 was crushed by the army. 55 of the protesters were killed.

⬆ Walter Ulbricht, leader of the SED from 1953 to 1971.

B

Total control over means of communication

The SED controlled communication and censored the media. The *Neues Deutschland* was the main newspaper and endorsed all party decisions. Television programmes gave positive messages about the state. However, many people watched Western TV and listened to Western radio from the FRG, giving them a different version of events.

> **Think**
>
> What is the message of this poster?

⬆ Propaganda posters were also frequently used throughout East Germany, like the one above, which celebrates Labour Day in 1955. The text roughly translates to 'ready to work and defend the homeland'.

C

Control of the economy

East Germany had a centrally planned economy. This meant the state ran nearly all the businesses and controlled the production of goods. People were given strict targets to meet and on the whole the economy did function well.

In shops people were restricted in what they could buy. They were often only given the option of buying East German goods as Western brands were banned.

D

Police using terror as a control tactic

The Ministry for State Security, commonly known as the Stasi, were the secret police. Their job was to monitor the people, spy on potential **agitators** and suppress any opposition. By 1989 there were 90,000 Stasi employees to watch over a population of 17 million, that's one spy per 200 people! In addition to this, the Stasi employed over 170,000 unofficial **informants**, so there was always a good chance that your neighbours could be spying on you.

⬆ When the Stasi interrogated people they put special cloths on the seats to collect the sweat of those being interviewed, so they could use dogs to find them later if necessary. After the fall of the Wall hundreds of thousands of 'smell jars' were found.

⬆ The Stasi used elaborate disguises to spy on the East Sterman people.

⬆ The Stasi used the latest technology to listen in on the German people. They placed listening devices in all manner of places, including suitcases, cars and walls, and even managed to incude a Tessina camera in this watch.

The Revisionist interpretation – East Germany the socialist dream?

Towards the middle of the 1990s a new interpretation gained popularity. Many ex-East Germans missed East Germany and began arguing that it had actually been a good place to live. In Germany a term to describe this, *Ostalgie*, came into use, a combination of the words *Ost* (East in German) and *nostalgia* (a sentimental longing for a period in the past).

As a communist country East Germany was trying to create a socialist dream where people were equal, worked together and helped each other in harmony. Read the next two pages to see if they achieved this.

E

Work

In East Germany there was no unemployment, everyone had a job. This meant that the government did not need to provide benefits at all. As the state was run 'by the workers and farmers under the leadership of the Communist Party' the workers had a lot more power than they would have had in a capitalist country. Any worker could leave their job with just two weeks' notice and it was virtually impossible to be sacked! Workers were encouraged to constructively criticise their employers and a culture of writing complaint letters spread through society.

Instead of having famous people appear on stamps, ➡ in the DDR workers appeared in pride of place.

F

⬆ A Trabant car.

Lifestyle

In some ways life in East Germany was simple. Often there was not a variety of products to purchase, for example there was only one car available, the Trabant. It was not very reliable and was only a little more powerful than a modern lawnmower. This lack of variety helped to provide equality amongst the majority of the population. Consumer goods, like televisions, were often difficult to get hold of and involved a long waiting list. But when they came, there was mass excitement. Crime levels in East Germany were extremely low compared to the West. Murder, rape and drug offences were scarce and people felt safe. When Germany reunited this changed and people found the change difficult.

G

Women

As the East German state believed in equality they heavily promoted women's rights. Women were encouraged into work and to be independent. This idea was boosted in the media and by propaganda posters. Abortion was made legal in East Germany four years earlier than in West Germany, giving women greater control over family planning.

However, the state also acknowledged the role of women as mothers. Lots of time was provided for maternity leave and if you were over 40 and married you would be given a day off every month to do your housework! Working mothers were supported with state child care being free, unlike the West where this was not the case.

⬆ Women in an East German factory.

H

Youth

The school week ran from Monday to Saturday, with a traditional curriculum that included compulsory lessons in Russian so children were ready to talk to their communist allies. Finland borrowed many East German education ideas and now has one of the best education systems in the world.

Outside of school there were many youth organisations. The Young Pioneers (ages 6–14) and the Free German Youth (ages 14–25) were the youth

organisations of the SED party and about 75 per cent of children were members. Similar to the Scouts they took part in outdoor activities, but in contrast they also learnt about the greatness of communism.

⬆ Television had children's programmes. *Sandmannchen* (or Sandman in English) was very popular. He rode in a rocket and often visited Moscow to meet other communist friends.

Enquiry Step 3: Developing your answer

1 Below are facts about the context of these two interpretations (that the DDR was a dictatorship and that the DDR was a nice place to live (a Socialist Dream)). Match the correct context to the correct interpretation. This will enable you to think about WHY they came about at different times.
   a) A lot of evidence about East Germany at this time had come from those people who had escaped because they hated the country or had been harassed by the Stasi.
   b) This interpretation was mostly held by ex-East Germans still living in what had been East Germany.
   c) This was a time of German reunification. The changes for East Germans were massive and daunting.
   d) This interpretation was largely formed after East Germany fell, when people were no longer facing the negative aspects of the state. This interpretation was strongly held by the West.
   e) This was the time of the **Cold War**. The West wanted to belittle communism and make it look cruel.
   f) This interpretation was formed while East Germany still existed and people hadn't had time to reflect on all aspects of it.
   (See answers on page 139.)
2 Now, working in pairs, discuss WHY each interpretation came about when it did.
3 Go back to your initial answer from Step 2 on page 109. Do you want to change it?

The post-revisionist interpretation – East Germany the 'people's paradox'

The previous two interpretations were quite subjective, meaning they were influenced by politics, personal feelings or opinions. However, post-2000, more objective post-revisionist interpretations emerged. In 2005 Professor Mary Fulbrook published her book on East Germany, *The People's State*. In the conclusion she says:

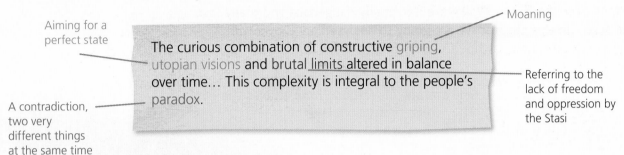

Moaning

Aiming for a perfect state

The curious combination of constructive griping, utopian visions and brutal limits altered in balance over time… This complexity is integral to the people's paradox.

Referring to the lack of freedom and oppression by the Stasi

A contradiction, two very different things at the same time

In essence she is saying that East Germany was a complicated mixture of ideas and experiences happening at once. This later and more balanced interpretation has emerged because there has been more time for a wealth of evidence to be collected, which Professor Fulbrook was able to access.

> **Think**
>
> Why do history teachers hate it when students say 'historians can't be accurate as they weren't there at the time'?

Enquiry Step 4: Concluding your enquiry

1 Revisit your initial hypothesis for the final time. Discuss what you now think with a partner.

2 Now you are going to write an essay on the enquiry question:

How and why have interpretations of life in East Germany changed so much in the last fifty years?

The essay needs three paragraphs, one for each interpretation you have studied. In each paragraph describe WHAT the interpretation was and WHO it came from using evidence from pages 108–112 and then explain WHY it came about at that time.

Finally, add a conclusion summarising your overall ideas about why interpretations have changed so much.

3 At the end of this section (page 118) you are going to be asked to create a museum about East Germany. How would you represent the 'people's paradox' in a museum? Discuss this with a partner.

How realistic is Paul Dowswell's account of escape?

Between 1961 and 1989, more than 600,000 East Germans fled to the West. Of these, 240,000 made illegal escapes, 40,000 crossing the Berlin Wall. Most left for economic reasons in hope of a better life, some went for political reasons having been hounded by the Stasi and some went for personal reasons to be reunited with family or friends.

Escapes over the Berlin Wall were extremely dangerous and many lost their lives. In this chapter we are going to analyse Paul Dowswell's fictional account of an escape from his book *Sektion 20*.

In Paul's book the main character, Alex Ostermann, is followed, arrested and tortured by the Stasi. One evening his father, Frank, makes the decision to leave the DDR. They enlist professionals to help them and are told to come to a factory which exports porcelain to the West…

Their means of escape stood before them – a big Mercedes four wheeler with a separate driver's compartment and a large cargo container with rear-opening doors. …

There was a little compartment right at the front of the container – like a false bottom on a suitcase, only upright and stretching from the floor to the ceiling. 'Good thing none of you are fat,' said the driver brusquely. There was just enough space for the four of them, if they put their little bags between their feet and squashed up shoulder to shoulder. The compartment door clicked into place and they were left in darkness.

'I hope I can breathe OK in here,' said Gretchen [his mother].

'No talking,' said the driver from the other side of the door.

Now the Ostermanns lived in a world of sound. Alex could feel his heart beating hard in his chest…

…The rear doors slammed shut. 'Now we're going,' whispered Frank….

The engine spluttered into life and the whole vehicle began to vibrate and tremble. 'Off you go,' someone shouted and they were buffeted to and fro as the vehicle turned into the street. It was disconcerting, feeling motion that you could not see. Alex began to feel a bit nauseous – and prayed he would not be sick.

The journey to Sonnenallee was mercifully brief. There was very little traffic at that time of night. Within five minutes the lorry engine stopped again. The driver and border guards exchanged pleasantries. Their voices were so close Alex felt as if he was standing next to them. In the silence he worried that even their breathing would give them away. …

…The engine burst into life again, sending a tremor through the whole vehicle. Alex had to bite his lip to stop himself cheering. They were on their way. He tried to picture the scene outside. The lorry moving between the flat open ground of the checkpoint and on towards the Western barrier under heavy arc lamps that cast stark black shadows. In a few seconds they would be on the other side.

Someone was shouting. What was being said over the noise of the engine was impossible to hear. A sudden rattle of machine-gun fire made them all flinch and try to make their bodies smaller – but there was no space to crouch. Alex heard Gretchen stifle a terrified scream. They stood stiff and upright in their little space, feeling intensely vulnerable. The next few seconds would decide their fate. The lorry stopped with a squeal of brakes and rattle of crockery. There was more shouting. A cabin door creaked open and slammed. The driver yelled at the border guards in an angry, panicky voice.

Then there were more shots. A man screamed in pain. The lorry shook a little as the other driver got out and there was the sound of running. A further burst of machine-gun fire followed and a shattering of porcelain as a stray bullet penetrated the cargo hold close to where they stood. Alex was so frightened it took a supreme effort not to wet himself.

There was silence, then, again, the sound of boots running on tarmac. Voices came over from the Western side. And footsteps. A heated exchange – a man explaining forcibly that the lorry was on the Western side of the border now and they were going to take it further. Then there were other voices. A guard explaining that the drivers had brandished guns and threatened them. That was why they had opened fire from the East, he said.

Even in their dark world Alex could not believe that….

…The lorry rocked a little as someone climbed into the cab. The engine started and they drove on for a short while. When they stopped, Frank and Gretchen began calling out for help. It took fifteen minutes for the lorry to be emptied sufficiently for the compartment to be opened. The door slid open and they were confronted by three men peering at them with anxious faces. Although he expected as much, it was a huge relief for Alex to see they were wearing the uniform of the West German Federal Defence Force.

Frank managed a startled grin. 'Guten Tag!' he said and put out his hand. 'Thank you for rescuing us.'

Alex staggered out into the cold night air and bright lights that hurt his eyes. They were on the edge of the border crossing – it stretched back to the Eastern side, all flat concrete road, wide and open on all sides. Over in the distant Eastern checkpoint buildings there was no one to be seen. He was drenched in sweat and immediately began to shiver. Four West German guards were walking towards them with two stretchers. The bodies they carried were both covered by blankets. Alex turned his back on his family and was violently sick.

Activity

1 In this extract Paul is trying to convey that escaping East Germany was a dangerous and scary experience. In pairs find the sentences where he makes the reader really feel this tension. Why might he emphasise this particular interpretation?

2 Paul very carefully sets this piece in East Germany in 1972. How does he let the reader know where they are and when they are? Find evidence in the extract.

3 Your answers to Questions 1 and 2 will have established how the author made his story *realistic*. As a class have a discussion about what evidence you would need to find out if his account is *accurate*.

Activity

4 Your challenge is to see if Paul has done his job properly! Make a list of similarities and differences between Paul's account and the real-life escapes (A–E) on the next two pages.

When I write historical fiction I try to be as real as possible. I want someone who lived through the era to say 'Yes, it was like that'.

Think

Everybody's experiences are different to some extent. Before you study pages 116–117, try to suggest some ways we might find out if the differences are realistic or not.

 A

Unusual methods of escape

Lots of people escaped in converted cars or by using fake documents. The border guards looked out for this so some took a more creative approach...

1963 Harry Deterling drove a train through the Wall

1963 Horst Klein, a trapeze artist, used a power cable as a tightrope

1966 Hartmut Richter swam across where a canal was used instead of the Wall

1979 Hans Strelczyk and family floated over in a balloon

1983 Michael Becker and Holger Bethke took a zip wire across

1989 the Holger brothers went back for their third brother in an ultra-light plane

B

Conrad Schumann

Two days after the Berlin border had been closed Conrad Schumann, an East German guard, saw his opportunity. Ditching his gun, Schumann leapt over the barbed wire to the West.

C

Ingrid's Escape

Leslie Collitt describes helping his fiancée Ingrid to escape in 1964 by using his sister's passport illegally.

Ingrid opened her handbag to take out my sister's passport. She was about to hand it to the guard when it fell out of her hands to the ground. Instantaneously, the three of us dived down to pick up the passport....

He studied the passport photo of my sister, glanced at Ingrid, and did the same with me. Then he uttered two words, the ones we most longed to hear: 'Auf Wiedersehen.' [goodbye]

As if in a trance, we walked to the border, which was lined with tank barriers and rolls of barbed wire on both sides, leaving a narrow opening for pedestrians. ... The tension had been so great that we were unable to utter a word.

D

Tunnel 57

Tunnel 57 was dug under the Wall by students and was one of the most successful escape attempts. It was very dangerous and the Stasi had already imprisoned a number of students when previous attempts had failed.

(57 people escaped through it.)

E

Deaths at the Wall

Although there is a lot of disagreement about the exact number of deaths there were at least 138 people who were killed or died at the Wall.

One of the first deaths was Peter Fechter. Peter and a friend jumped the Eastern Wall and ran into the death strip, the area before the Western Wall. The Eastern guards shot Peter in the pelvis before he could climb the Western Wall. The Western guards were not allowed to go on to the death strip to help him and the Eastern guards left him there to die.

Activity

5 Hopefully you agree that Paul's account is pretty realistic. In fact, he describes it as 'not super dramatic'. Why would he choose not to make it as unusual as some of the other escapes on this page?

6 How useful is historical fiction, like Paul's? Would you include this in a museum of East Germany?

7 Make a list of the key facts about escaping from East Germany that you would want to include in your museum.

What would you include in a museum about East Germany?

So far in this section (pages 106–117) we have analysed other people's interpretations, whether they be academic or pieces of historical fiction. In this last chapter you are going to develop your own interpretation! Your challenge will be to design a mini museum about East Germany. Read the text on page 119 before starting the activity below.

Activity

You have become the curator of a mini museum about East Germany. Most museums have a large store room where they keep the artefacts that are not currently on display. In the middle of this page is a store room full of objects relating to East Germany. They have all been mentioned somewhere on pages 106–117.

1 Your museum exhibition space is very small so you can only pick FIVE artefacts. Choose the ones that you think best represent the history of East Germany.

2 All objects in museums have information labels. Write the labels for your five objects. Explain what they are and, more importantly, what they tell us about East Germany.

3 Get into a group. Compare your choices with the others in your group. Were your objects the same as the others'? What does this tell you about interpretations in museums?

4 Now let's make this harder. Imagine other museums from different times and different places but with the exact same store room to choose objects from. What do you think the curators of these museums would have chosen? Complete Activity 1 again for each scenario:

> Scenario A: The museum is located in Bonn, the capital of West Germany in 1970. At this time relations between East and West Germany were tense and the capitalists were horrified about what was happening in East Germany.

> Scenario B: The museum is located in Moscow, the capital of the Soviet Union, in 1980. At this time communism was beginning to fail so the Soviets wanted to highlight its successes.

> Scenario C: The museum is located in Berlin, the capital of reunified Germany, in 2005.

5 Discuss with a partner. What factors influenced your decision in each scenario?

a) Fragment of the Berlin Wall

b) Trabant car

c) Scarf from the Young Pioneers

d) Photo of Walter Ulbricht

e) Stasi listening device

f) Sandmannchen doll

g) Copy of Sektion 20

h) Flag of the Socialist Unity Party

i) SED Propaganda poster

j) Smell jar

k) Photo of East German women working

l) Hans Strelczyk's hot air balloon

m) Car converted for escape

n) Photo of Conrad Schumann

o) Stasi disguise

Think

If you had space for one more item in Activities 1 and 4, and could choose anything you wanted from East Germany, what would you include?

Museum exhibitions offer an interpretation of the past themselves. The **curators** pick artefacts and display them in a way that will educate people. They obviously cannot include everything as space is limited and they only have access to a limited selection of artefacts. However, by careful selection they emphasise parts of history that they believe to be relevant or important, thus making it an interpretation of the past.

Think

Why are there sometimes different interpretations of the past? Explain your answer by referring to the differing histories.

Why was 9/11 so important?

While studying history you have probably realised that religion has played an enormous part in making things happen. Perhaps you remember the story of the Gunpowder Plotters, men who were prepared to use violence to bring about religious change. Rulers and ordinary people have often been deeply motivated by their religious beliefs. However, when we were deciding what to include in this book (1901 to the present day), it was tempting to forget about religion. Communist governments rejected religion and the terrible suffering brought about by the First and Second World Wars seemed to leave little room for God. Yet, religion had not gone away and continues to have a huge impact on the modern world.

On 11 September 2001, nineteen **al-Qaeda** terrorists hijacked four planes, crashing them into the World Trade Center and the Pentagon. By the end of the day 3,000 people had lost their lives. The men who carried out these attacks claimed to be acting for religious reasons, defending Islam from the United States and the Western world.

> **Think**
> The terrorists could not destroy the United States in a military attack. Why did they target the World Trade Center and the Pentagon? What do you think they were trying to achieve?

A

⬆ The attack on the World Trade Center, 11 September 2001. The Twin Towers, as the centrepieces of the World Trade Center, symbolised America's economic power and prosperity. The Pentagon, as the headquarters for the US Department of Defense, serves as a symbol of American military power, and was attacked on the same day.

The 'war on terror'

After the attacks there was worldwide shock at the destruction and loss of life. There was also great sympathy for the American people, not least from Islamic leaders who condemned the actions of al-Qaeda. The US government declared a 'war on terror', the events and consequences of which are outlined in Map B below. Their number one target was Osama bin Laden, the leader of al-Qaeda, who was based in Afghanistan. You will find out more about bin Laden, al-Qaeda and Afghanistan on pages 124–127.

B

October 2001: a US-led attack, supported by 58 different countries, was launched on Afghanistan to drive out al-Qaeda. By December, al-Qaeda forces had fled to Pakistan or fallen back to their well-protected strongholds in the mountains.

2002: US President George W Bush strongly criticised Iraq for supporting 'terror'. There was a suspicion that Saddam Hussein, the Iraqi leader, was involved in 9/11, though this turned out to be completely untrue.

In 2014: a group calling itself Islamic State, and appearing even more extreme than al-Qaeda, took control of large areas of Iraq and Syria.

2003: a US-led invasion of Iraq toppled Saddam Hussein from power. The invasion was supported by 46 other countries, including the UK, in a 'Coalition of the Willing'.

2011: Bin Laden was tracked down in Pakistan and killed by US Navy SEALS. However, the high profile of al-Qaeda had already inspired other Islamic terror groups in areas as diverse as the Middle East, Africa, Indonesia and the Philippines.

By 2004: the situation was violent and chaotic. US and coalition forces were unpopular and many al-Qaeda trained fighters went to Iraq to fight them. In 2010, US forces left Iraq but the violence continued and Iraq proved to be an unstable state.

The world since 9/11

Since 2001 there have been no terror attacks to match the sophistication and scale of 9/11. However, attacks by **Islamist** terrorists have continued across the world. These have hit countries such as Bali, India, Nigeria, Spain, France, Iraq, Kenya and the United Kingdom – with the total death toll well into the thousands.

Activity

1 In small groups or pairs, discuss what questions you have about the attack on 9/11. Make a list of these and try to answer them as you work through the rest of this section.
2 Look carefully at the information on pages 120–121. How effective has the 'war on terror' been? Give your reasons.

⬆ Wreckage after the London bombings, 7 July 2005. In 2005, 52 civilians and four British-born suicide bombers died in London. The bombers were angry about British support for the invasions of Afghanistan and Iraq and the treatment of Muslims around the world.

Was religion the cause of the 9/11 attacks?

On pages 120–121 you saw that the 9/11 attacks have had a big effect on recent history. To many in the Western world, bin Laden's motives seemed clear. His speeches and videotaped broadcasts talked in terms of 'jihad' (holy war) against the 'crusaders' and 'infidels' (non-believers). On the face of it, al-Qaeda was fighting a holy war for religious reasons.

If you are to understand the causes for al-Qaeda's actions you need to go back much further than the events of 9/11. By reading the information on pages 122–127 you should be able decide how important a role religion played in motivating bin Laden and al-Qaeda. Was 9/11 simply part of a 'holy war' or were there other underlying causes?

Activity

1 In pairs or small groups, discuss what effect the existence of Israel and the Palestinian issue had on the thinking of Osama bin Laden and al-Qaeda. Identify the religious, political and other reasons that motivated them.

2 You are going to use a concept map to show the causes behind the 9/11 attacks. Write '9/11' in the middle of a large sheet of paper.

▪ Write the factor headings 'Religion', 'Politics' and 'Other' around the outside.

▪ Add the religious, political and other reasons you identified in Activity 1. Remember to break the information down into smaller chunks before adding it to the correct place on your concept map.

▪ You may want replace 'Other' with your own heading as you find out more.

1948: The creation of Israel

Palestine had been home to the Jews for around 1,200 years, but they were forced to leave in AD 70 (see page 46). From the seventh century Muslim Arabs had settled it and made it their own. By the twentieth century, however, many Jews wanted their own homeland, safe from the anti-Semitism they faced elsewhere. These Jews called themselves Zionists. Following the Holocaust (see pages 46–61), the pressure for a Jewish homeland increased.

In 1948, the new Jewish state of Israel came into being, splitting the land in Palestine between the Arab and Jewish populations (see map on page 123). Fighting broke out and by the end of 1948 Israel was in control of 80 per cent of the land. Three-quarters of a million Palestinian Arabs became refugees living in neighbouring states. The rest remained in the new state of Israel as a minority people.

> **Think**
>
> Why do you think the Holocaust increased Zionist pressure for a Jewish homeland?

1967: The Six-Day War

After 1948, Israel faced hostility from the Arab world. They refused to recognise it as a state and condemned Israel's treatment of the Palestinians. In 1967, following a victory in the Six-Day War against Egypt, Syria, Jordan and Iraq, Israel controlled land in Sinai, the Gaza Strip and the West Bank (see Map A). The Palestinians who lived in these areas faced work and travel restrictions. There was a heavy Israeli security presence and thousands of Palestinians who were seen as security risks had their homes pulled down. These occupied territories have remained under Israeli control.

> **Think**
>
> After the 9/11 attacks, some Palestinians took to the streets with pictures of Osama bin Laden to celebrate. Why might this have been?

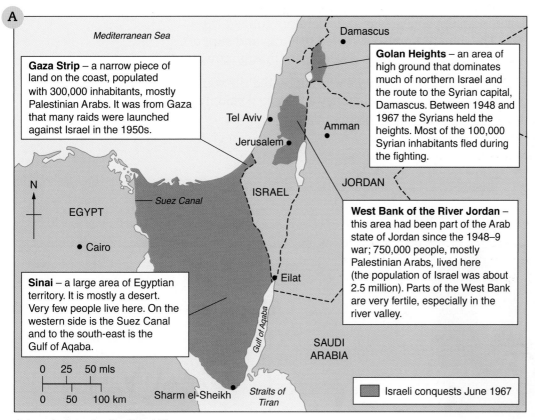

A

Gaza Strip – a narrow piece of land on the coast, populated with 300,000 inhabitants, mostly Palestinian Arabs. It was from Gaza that many raids were launched against Israel in the 1950s.

Golan Heights – an area of high ground that dominates much of northern Israel and the route to the Syrian capital, Damascus. Between 1948 and 1967 the Syrians held the heights. Most of the 100,000 Syrian inhabitants fled during the fighting.

West Bank of the River Jordan – this area had been part of the Arab state of Jordan since the 1948–9 war; 750,000 people, mostly Palestinian Arabs, lived here (the population of Israel was about 2.5 million). Parts of the West Bank are very fertile, especially in the river valley.

Sinai – a large area of Egyptian territory. It is mostly a desert. Very few people live here. On the western side is the Suez Canal and to the south-east is the Gulf of Aqaba.

Israeli conquests June 1967

⬆ Israel after the Six-Day War.

Today, thousands of Palestinian families still live in refugee camps with little hope of returning to their homes. Many Palestinians and some of Israel's Arab neighbours accuse the Israelis of stealing land from the Muslim population. From its earliest days, Israel was supported by the USA, who supplied it with money and equipment. Today, Israel receives millions of dollars in military aid from the USA and is one of the strongest powers in the Middle East.

B

The expansion of Israel is one of the greatest crimes, and you are the leaders of its criminals. And of course there is no need to explain and prove the degree of American support for Israel. The creation of Israel is a crime that must be erased.

Osama bin Laden's 'Letter to America', 2002.

1979 – The Soviet Union invades Afghanistan

In 1979, the Soviet Union invaded Afghanistan, sparking a war that would last until they withdrew in 1989. The Soviets moved into Afghanistan to protect the communist government, which was under threat from Muslim tribal leaders. Those resisting the Soviets called themselves **mujahidin**, a word meaning holy warrior, to show they were engaged in the struggle to protect Islam.

Foreign involvement

This was during the **Cold War**, a time in which the USA and Soviet Union were hostile to each other's interests. The Americans hoped the Soviets would get bogged down in an expensive war and therefore funded the mujahidin generously. The mujahidin also received funding and support from Saudi Arabia, which wanted an Islamic government in Afghanistan.

Osama bin Laden was one of many young Saudis who supported the war effort against the Soviets. At first he provided money and helped volunteers reach Afghanistan, but soon he became a mujahidin fighter himself.

⬆ Osama bin Laden, leader of al-Qaeda until his death in 2011. Bin Laden ordered the attacks on 9/11 and several other high profile operations. He was born in Saudi Arabia in 1957, the son of a billionaire businessman. In 1979, Osama went to Afghanistan to fight the Soviet forces. He formed al-Qaeda in 1988.

⬆ Front cover of *The Red Cancer*, Abdul Azzam's book attacking communism. Azzam was a radical preacher whose ideas influenced bin Laden and many of those who went to fight in Afghanistan.

E

Think

Money and training from the USA and Saudi Arabia allowed the mujahidin to buy and use weaponry like that shown in Photo E. How might this have posed risks in the future?

⬆ Mujahidin anti-aircraft emplacement, Afghanistan, 1984. The mujahedin were well armed and used guerrilla tactics to attack the Soviets. The war proved extremely costly for the Soviet Union, both in terms of lives lost and money spent. In 1989 the Soviets pulled out.

The birth of al-Qaeda

Al-Qaeda was formed in 1988, and grew out of the network of foreign mujahidin in Afghanistan. It aimed to rid Muslim countries of outside influence. Many volunteer mujahidin were influenced by the ideas of radical Muslim preachers who argued that Islam was under attack not only from communism but also from Western values. They encouraged the idea of **martyrdom**, saying that fighters who were killed defending Islam would go to Paradise when they died.

Think

How does the idea of martyrdom help explain the actions of the terrorists in the 9/11 attacks, London bombings and other suicide attacks?

The war in Afghanistan gave a whole generation of Arab mujahadin battlefield experience and the confidence that they could achieve their aims elsewhere. By the end of the conflict, a new enemy had emerged – America. The USA was accused of propping up Arab states that had become corrupted by Western ideas and were not religious enough. Therefore, it was the duty of the mujahadin to fight growing American influence and help restore these countries to a stricter Islamic rule.

Activity

3 In pairs or small groups, discuss the effect that the war in Afghanistan had on the thinking of Osama bin Laden and al-Qaeda. Identify the religious, political and other reasons that motivated them.

4 Add to the concept map that you started on page 122. Remember to break the information down into smaller chunks before adding it to the correct place on your concept map.

1990–91 – The Gulf War

In August 1990, Saddam Hussein, the Iraqi leader, invaded Kuwait. His actions threatened neighbouring Saudi Arabia and risked disrupting the world's oil supply. Therefore, a US-led coalition, including Britain and many other countries, took decisive action. Bases were quickly established in Saudi Arabia to ensure a **'no fly zone'** over southern Iraq. When ground fighting began in January 1991, it took just five weeks for coalition forces to drive the Iraqi army from Kuwait.

Around 5,000 US personnel remained based in Saudi Arabia from 1990 until 2003. Bin Laden, who in 1990 had had left Afghanistan and returned to Saudi Arabia, was furious, as were many other Muslims in the region.

In 1990, Saudi Arabia was divided. Some Saudis wished to modernise the country while others, like bin Laden, wanted a strict observance of traditional Muslim beliefs. Bin Laden strongly criticised the ruling royal family of Saudi Arabia, claiming that they were too influenced by Western ideas. In 1994, he was expelled from Saudi Arabia and after some time in Sudan found his way back to Afghanistan.

> **Think**
>
> Look at Photo F. How does it help explain why bin Laden was angry that American soldiers were based in Saudi Arabia?

F

◄ Muslim pilgrims walk around the sacred Ka'bah in the Prophet's Mosque in Mecca, Saudi Arabia. It is the duty of every Muslim to make a pilgrimage to Mecca at least once in their lifetime. It is the most sacred place in the Muslim world.

G

The United States has been occupying the lands of Islam in the holiest of places, the Arabian Peninsula, plundering its riches, dictating to its rulers, humiliating its people, terrorising its neighbours, and turning the Peninsula into a spearhead through which to fight the neighbouring Muslim peoples.

Osama bin Laden, 1997.

> **Think**
>
> Look at Extract G. Were bin Laden's concerns about the presence of American troops just about religion?

The return to Afghanistan, 1996

In 1996, Osama bin Laden returned to Afghanistan. The country was now under the control of the Taliban, which ran it along strictly religious lines.

In 1998, from his new base in Afghanistan, bin Laden approved the bombing of US Embassies in Kenya and Tanzania. In response, the Americans launched cruise missile strikes on al-Qaeda sites in Afghanistan and Sudan. Bin Laden was now at the top of America's 'most wanted' list.

By early 1999, bin Laden and his advisers were working on what they called the 'planes operation'. This was the plan that formed the basis of the 9/11 attacks in 2001. Of the 19 hijackers involved, 15 were from Saudi Arabia. They were clearly deeply religious and convinced that their actions would make them martyrs, granting them a place in paradise when they died.

The historical debate

Historians have continued to disagree about the causes of the 9/11 attacks and the actions of al-Qaeda.

In 2004, British journalist and Middle East expert Jason Burke wrote,

> [Osama bin Laden's] agenda is basically a political one, though it is couched, of course, in religious language and imagery.

In 2005, historian David Starkey was interviewed about the Gunpowder Plot of 1605. His comments compared the Catholic plotters to modern Islamic terrorists such as those who carried out the attacks on 9/11.

> The parallels between the actions of the plotters and modern-day terrorists are terrifying and the motivation is the same – that religion is the only important thing and that if the Government does not subscribe to the idea that your religion is absolute it must be removed.

> **Think**
>
> How do Starkey and Burke disagree about the causes of 9/11?

Activity

5 In pairs or small groups, discuss the effect the Gulf War and events in Saudi Arabia had on the thinking of Osama bin Laden and al-Qaeda. Identify the religious, political and other reasons that motivated them.

6 Add to the concept map that you started on page 122. Remember to break the information down into smaller chunks before adding it around the correct part of your concept map.

7 Look at your concept map. Draw lines to the middle from each of the factors you have identified. Use a thick, bold line for the most important factors, and a thin, faint line for the less important factors.

8 Next, look for links between the factors themselves. Draw any links using the same method as in 7, depending on how strong you think the links are.

9 Now it is time for you to make up your own mind. Do you agree with Starkey – that religion was the cause of the 9/11 attacks – or do you agree with Jason Burke that al-Qaeda's agenda was a political one?

A sense of period

The aim of all the books in this series is the same – to leave you with 'a sense of period'.

The activities on this spread will help you decide how well we have done in this book in leaving you with a 'sense of period' for the twentieth century.

	Middle Ages, 1066–1509	Early Modern Era, 1509–1745
A	Norman Conquest, Magna Carta, Black Death	Reformation, Glorious Revolution, Union with Scotland
B	William I, Edward I, Edward III	Henry VIII, Oliver Cromwell, William of Orange
C	Peasants' Revolt	The Armada
D	Murder of Thomas Becket	Execution of Charles I
E	Royal rulers, rebellions and the beginning of Parliament	King or Parliament?
F	A time of disease and warfare	A time of religion and politics

Activity

1 We started the book (pages 2–3) by suggesting that the 'defining event of the period' was Hiroshima. Would you have chosen Hiroshima? If not, suggest some other events which, for you, better illustrate the age.

2 On pages 8–9 we listed our suggestions of eleven important events of the period. Do you agree?

3 We divided your studies into different themes – 'An age of warfare', 'Britain' and 'The post-war world'. Look back and review your learning in each of these sections. Each one will have helped to create your 'sense of period', but which aspects most dominate your impression of the times?

4 As you saw on page 5, Walter G Moss called the twentieth century 'an age of progress?' (*with* the question mark). Having studied this textbook, what would you call the twentieth century: the 'Age of ___'?

The years 1745–1901	Modern Age, 1901–present
Industrial Revolution, French Revolution, Ireland	Activity 5a
I.K. Brunel, Charles Darwin, Lord Shaftesbury	Activity 5b
The abolition of the slave trade	Activity 5c
The early industrialists	Activity 5d
The coming of democracy	Activity 5e
A time of technological and medical advance	Activity 5f

Activity

5 Debate and take a class vote to choose the key aspects of the period:
   a the three most important events of the period
   b the three most important people of the period
   c the most interesting topic
   d the 'defining event'
   e the most important issue(s) in government
   f Choose two or three words which, for you, together sum up the twentieth century; make them into a sentence which starts with the words: 'A time of…' and which 'sums up the age'. Share your sentence with other groups, and use their comments and ideas to refine your own sentence.

6 Compare your impressions of the twentieth century with the sense of period you have previously formed about the other eras of history you have studied. In what ways was the twentieth century different from, and similar to, the previous ages of history you have studied?

Britain's changing landscape

Britain's landscape has changed greatly through the millennia.

This section will study this, by asking you to research how the landscape changed in your own local area.

We will begin by reminding ourselves of some key features of the British landscape which we have mentioned so far in this series of textbooks.

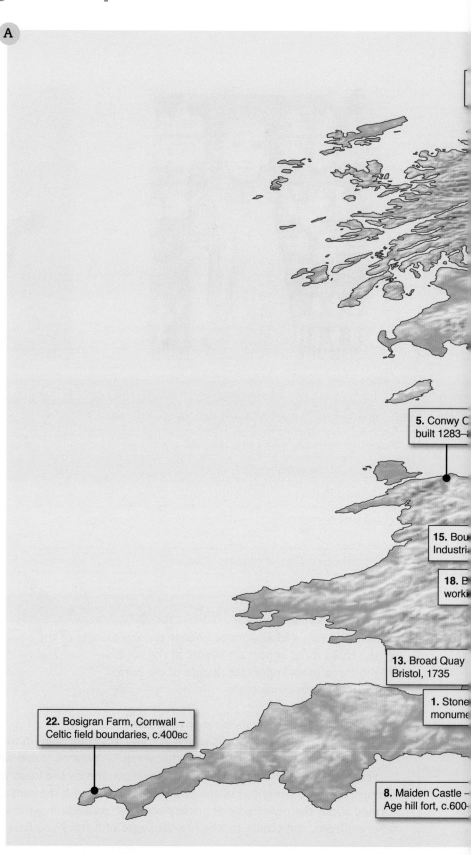

A

5. Conwy C
built 1283–

15. Bou
Industria

18. B
worki

13. Broad Quay
Bristol, 1735

1. Stone
monume

22. Bosigran Farm, Cornwall –
Celtic field boundaries, c.400BC

8. Maiden Castle –
Age hill fort, c.600–

Activity

1. Draw a timeline 3000BC–AD2000, and mark the 25 places shown on the map on to it. Discuss as a class if you know of any important **heritage** landscape features the map has missed.
2. Select SIX significant places and design a 'fly-over' tour of Britain to illustrate 'Britain's changing landscape through the ages' for an imaginary TV programme.
3. Sort the 25 places into 'economic', 'social', 'military' and 'religious' features.

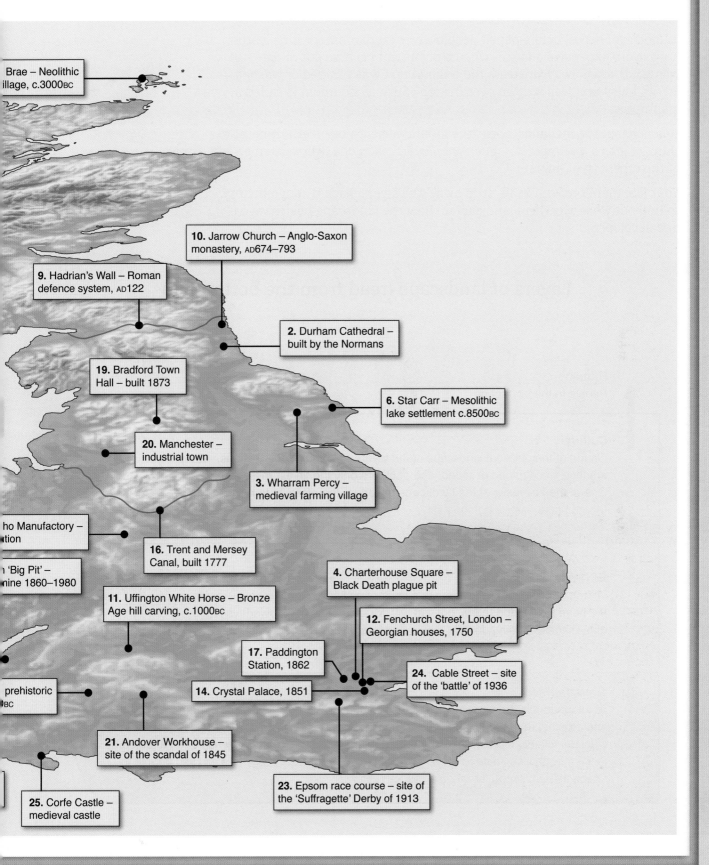

Brae – Neolithic illage, c.3000BC

10. Jarrow Church – Anglo-Saxon monastery, AD674–793

9. Hadrian's Wall – Roman defence system, AD122

2. Durham Cathedral – built by the Normans

19. Bradford Town Hall – built 1873

6. Star Carr – Mesolithic lake settlement c.8500BC

20. Manchester – industrial town

3. Wharram Percy – medieval farming village

ho Manufactory – tion

16. Trent and Mersey Canal, built 1777

4. Charterhouse Square – Black Death plague pit

'Big Pit' – nine 1860–1980

11. Uffington White Horse – Bronze Age hill carving, c.1000BC

12. Fenchurch Street, London – Georgian houses, 1750

17. Paddington Station, 1862

24. Cable Street – site of the 'battle' of 1936

prehistoric BC

14. Crystal Palace, 1851

21. Andover Workhouse – site of the scandal of 1845

23. Epsom race course – site of the 'Suffragette' Derby of 1913

25. Corfe Castle – medieval castle

Investigating the landscape

Now we are going to prepare for your study of the changing landscape in your area.

In medieval times, before paper, people wrote on parchment (fine leather). It was very expensive and so – when a document became out of date – it was not thrown away. Instead, the original text was scraped or washed off, and new text was written over the top. Such a document is called a 'palimpsest'.

When you study the landscape – 'the ground beneath our feet' – it helps to think of it as a 'palimpsest' – a series of layers, each one overwritten on top of the others (see Diagram A).

Your job, therefore, will be to 'strip away' the layers, back through history, to find out what was there, and explain how the landscape has changed and developed.

A

Layers of landscape (read from the bottom up)

Human
People in the landscape

Cultural
On top of the physical landscape stand layers of human constructions. Many are long since ruined or rotted, and of others only the tiniest relics remain. One of the key tasks of the landscape historian, therefore, is to notice and record these vestiges of the past.

Environmental
On top of the topography, there is a layer of ecology. Some of this is made up of the natural flora and fauna, but you will discover most of it nowadays is man-made – farming, forests, parks and gardens – and part of its history.

Topographical
At the bottom is the landform itself, shaped mainly by geological factors (bedrock, glaciation and erosion), but altered in places by human activity (such as burial mounds, quarries, cuttings, levees, etc.). Everything that has happened through history has been affected by this – though less so as time has gone on, as modern technology has allowed people to shape the landscape for themselves.

Starting your investigation

When town planners are conducting an archaeological survey for a planning site, they begin with what they call 'a desktop exercise' – a survey of what is already known and available about the designated area. That is how you should begin your study of your local landscape.

When you have done that, however, there is no substitute for 'field work' – going out into the area and researching for yourself.

 B

Out of the mists of time...

⬆ The ruins of Corfe Castle in Dorset date back to the eleventh century.

Think

1 No elements of the landscape are permanent, especially human impacts.
  a Which aspects of human activity are less likely to survive than others
  b How might this possibly distort our interpretation of the history of the landscape?
2 Nowadays, planning laws prevent developers destroying heritage features. Do you agree? Should we artificially preserve the inherited landscape in this way, or should we allow progress naturally to replace it?

Activity

Desktop survey
1 Define the area/boundaries of your chosen landscape study – not too large to investigate, but not so small that it contains no features of interest.
2 Construct a timeline of the important historical events in your chosen landscape area.
3 Make a list of all the key heritage features in the landscape.
4 Find an aerial photograph of the area. Note the FORM of the landscape – the hills and valleys, the moors, rivers and marshes.
5 Study old maps of the area – particularly old Ordnance Survey maps. Look for:
  ▌ Buildings – archaeological, public, domestic, industrial
  ▌ Spaces – public, private and shared – and their uses
  ▌ Boundaries – walls, building lines
  ▌ Links – roads, rivers and communications that are still visible in the landscape today.

Use the internet to gather relevant historical information about the features you have noticed – such as surveys (e.g. Domesday Book, 1187); nineteenth-century directories; reports of archaeological digs; paintings and photographs of the area; descriptions of the area in literature and poetry.

Field study/Site visits
1 Walk the area, finding the key features, and seeing if your theories and ideas work 'on the ground'. Take photos and annotate drawings to record your ideas.
2 Collect people's recollections and folk memories about the features in your identified area.

Investigating a local landscape – Newton Aycliffe

Before you write your own report of the historical development of the landscape in your area (see page 137), here is a study of the historic landscape around Newton Aycliffe in County Durham.

It will help you see the kinds of things you might watch out for in your own study.

2 Shackleton Beacon, an Iron Age Hill Fort.

4 The Stockton and Darlington Railway (1825) which took coal from the mines of the west to the docks on Teesside.

5 Modern private 'anywhere' housing estates.

6 Newton Aycliffe was built after 1945 as a flagship settlement for the Welfare State. Until the 1970s, all the houses were council houses.

7 1950s' **utility housing**.

1 Field boundaries, mostly enclosed in the 17th and 18th centuries.

3 19th-century railway workers' terrace housing

10 The Roman Road 'Dere Street' ran from York to Hadrian's Wall.

12 Redworth Hall: a manor house since Norman times, the façade was built in the 18th century.

14 Aycliffe Business Park: an ordnance factory was built here during the Second World War, and turned into an industrial estate after the war.

16 'The old A1' – the main north–south road, dating from medieval times. There was a 'toll house' here for an 18th-century 'turnpike' road (which charged users a toll).

11 Newbiggin, site of a medieval fortified manor house.

13 Heighington: a Norman planned village, built as a concentration camp and local administrative centre after William the Conqueror destroyed the area in 1069.

15 Aycliffe Church: 19th-century exterior, based on a Saxon church.

Activity

1 Put the 20 features in the diagram below onto a timeline; use it to construct a brief history of the landscape.

2 Sort the 20 features into the following categories – transport, economy and settlement. Use your lists to work out a brief history of each in the area.

3 In what ways has the landform affected the history of the area?

8 The modern motorway (built 1969) is technologically able to cross the marshy Carrs.

9 19th-century field boundaries, created when the Carrs were drained.

Key:

▬ Land to the west of this contour is higher, drier ground

▬ The Carrs: in 10,000BC this lowland area was a lake, and was often-flooded and boggy until the 19th century

A1(M)

Lime Lane

Bishopton

17 Site of a windmill dating from AD 1333.

18 Lime Lane: one of many narrow, windy roads in the area dating from Saxon times.

19 Remains of the failed medieval settlement at Heworth, with medieval 'ridge-and-furrow' plough marks,

20 Bishopton: site of a Norman 'motte and bailey' castle.

Interpreting the landscape

In Book 2 of this series, we introduced you to the idea that the way historians have presented history has changed a lot in the last half-century.

The same has happened in the study of the development of the landscape.

Traditional:

When they studied the history of the landscape in the 1950s, historical geographers such as H.C. Darby and W.G. Hoskins were very like the 'Whig' historians we introduced you to in Book 2. They believed that the landscape had evolved naturally and inevitably, and that all they had to do was to discover the 'truth' about how it had developed. If you write up your investigation as a narrative story, then this is the kind of history you will be writing.

Marxist:

By the 1960s, as in history, **Marxist** scholars were beginning to redefine historical geography. For them, the developing landscape was an outworking of social conflict between rich and poor, and they were concerned to find out how the evolving landscape mirrored changes in power, wealth and ownership. As you write up your report, as well as just what happened, you will wish to be explaining WHO changed the landscape, and WHY.

Poststructuralist:

More recently, the writing of landscape history has changed yet again. 'Poststructuralists' (equivalent to the 'post-revisionist' historians) have realised that 'landscape' has different meanings for different people – an economist will 'read' the landscape very differently to an historian, for instance. You will wish, therefore, to acknowledge in your report that several different landscapes can exist in the same place at the same time, and at least to define whose landscape you have been investigating.

You are now ready to begin to write your report on the development of the landscape in your local area.

Activity

1 Define your target audience (historians? tourists? incomers? children? etc.). This will determine WHAT you write in your report, and HOW you present it.

2 You may wish to divide the task as a class, with different groups of students taking different aspects (e.g. transport, economy and settlement), or areas of the landscape.

3 Discuss in a group the results of your desktop activity on page 133.
   a) Record what you have discovered about the landscape, including issues such as:
   ▮ when different features seem first to have appeared
   ▮ how the landscape has changed over time
   ▮ turning points in the landscape's history
   ▮ what the different features reveal about life at different periods of history.
   b) Make sure you EXPLAIN as well as describe the features, relating the changes in the landscape to such as:
   ▮ underlying landform – HOW it influenced what developed where
   ▮ historical events – WHAT happened, and WHO was in power at the time
   ▮ developments through time in economy and technology.
   c) Consider how RELIABLE your conclusions are – could there be alternative interpretations of the facts?

4 Support and refine your ideas, where possible, with the results of your field work and site visits.

5 Finally, write up your study, aiming it at the target audience, to report:
   First, a brief description of your landscape area.
   ▮ Then, an 'explained narrative' of the history of the landscape – focus on analysing the facts, weighing the evidence, and putting the changes in their historical context.
   ▮ Next, write separate summary-histories for transport, the economy and settlement in the area, as revealed in the landscape.
   ▮ A conclusion, in which you sum up the main developments in the local landscape, and the forces which drove those developments.

⬇ 'Several different landscapes can exist in the same place at the same time'. In this aerial view of the city of York, what would an historian see? What would a tourist see? Think of other people who would 'see' completely different things in this landscape.

Glossary

Abdicate When a king or queen gives up their right to rule.

Agitators A person who urges others to protest or rebel.

Al-Qaeda A world-wide network of terrorist groups which believed they were fighting a holy war (*jihad*) against the Americans, Israel and any countries that support the two.

Alliances An agreement between two countries to cooperate – often in trade agreements, usually promising military support.

Allies The alliance of Britain, the USA and the USSR, which fought together in the Second World War against the Axis (Germany, Japan and Italy).

Anarchists Political agitators who wish to reduce the power of the state to the minimum.

Annex To conquer/take over the government of an area or country.

Anti-Semitism Hatred of Jews.

Armistice An agreement to stop fighting in a war; a truce.

Arson Criminally setting fire to a building.

Aryan The Nazi name for the master race – ideally fair-haired, blue-eyed, physically superior and ruthless.

Axis The alliance of Germany, Japan and Italy, which fought together in the Second World War against the Allies (Britain, the USA and the USSR).

Blockade An act of sealing off a place to prevent goods or people from entering or leaving.

Bolsheviks A hard-left form of Marxism.

Boycott To refuse to trade with or buy goods from a country, company or shop, usually on moral grounds.

Census A counting of the population.

Civil war A war between two groups within a single country.

Cold War The conflict between the USA and the USSR, 1945–89, which never came to actual fighting (i.e. to 'hot war') because both sides feared it would be a nuclear war that could destroy all humanity.

Concentration camp A detention centre (e.g. in Nazi Germany) for criminals, political opponents or members of 'inferior' races.

Conscription 'Calling up' citizens to fight in the army.

Counter-culture A way of life that is different from the mainstream culture within which it operates.

Coup A sudden takeover of the government by a group within the government, without an election or revolution.

Crusades Originally medieval wars against Islam, the term 'crusade' has come to mean any ideological campaign.

Curator The person in charge of a museum who selects the objects for display.

Demilitarised An area where armed forces are not allowed to go.

Disposable income 'Take-home pay' – the money left to spend after meeting required deductions such as taxes, national insurance, pension contributions, etc.

Einsatzgruppen Death squads who rounded up and shot Jews in Eastern Europe.

Expansionism The desire of a country to grow and conquer other countries.

Duckboard The planks of wood placed in the bottom of the trenches.

Flogged A form of whipping/corporal punishment, often with a wooden birch stick.

Flying picket (See 'pickets'.)

Franchise The people who have the right to vote in an election.

Führer A German word meaning 'leader', which Hitler gave to himself as a title in August 1934. Hitler asserted that it joined into one his roles as Chancellor of the Government, as Supreme Commander of the Army, and as President of the State.

Gestapo The Nazi *Geheime Staatspolizei* – a secret state police.

Ghetto An area in a town or city where Jews were made to live.

Great Depression The longest, farthest-reaching economic depression of the twentieth century, which originated in the United States in 1929, but had a global impact, with most countries not recovering until the late 1930s.

Guerrilla Soldier who do not fight openly in pitched battles, but in irregular ways, such as sabotage, ambushes, assassinations, etc.

Heritage Those historical remains of our landscape and culture that are deemed to have value for today – for instance as tourist attractions, or as a record of the past.

Informants A person who spies on others and then passes information to the authorities.

Jihadist A combatant who believes they are fighting an holy war waged on behalf of Islam.

Kriegsmarine The German Navy 1935–45.

Left-wing A political point of view that supports social equality, and typically promotes progressive social values. 'Hard left' politicians are more extreme in their views than the 'moderate left' or 'centre left' (terms which might be used of Britain's Labour Party).

Luftwaffe The German Airforce 1935–45.

Malnutrition Undernourishment, short of starvation.

Martyrdom Dying – often intentionally – for one's religious faith.

Marxism A form of communism.

MI5 The UK's Military Intelligence (spy) service, with responsibility for counter-terrorism and domestic security.

Militant An activist who favours confrontational and violent methods.

Monarchists People who want a single ruler – e.g. a king or an emperor – as their ruler.

Mujahidin A word meaning 'holy warrior' used by those who believe they are fighting to protect Islam.

Nationalisation Where the government takes over the ownership and running of an industry (e.g. the railways, coal, electricity, water).

No fly zone An area patrolled by fighter jets to ensure that no foreign aircraft enter.

Oppression Unjust or cruel treatment.

Partition To divide something.

Passover A Jewish religious festival.

Patriotism Having or showing great support or love for your country.

Pickets Where striking workers set up outside their place of work and try to persuade other workers to join them in their strike. 'Secondary picketing' is where strikers try to persuade the employees of other firms/industries to join them. 'Flying pickets' are strikers who travel to places elsewhere in the country to mount pickets.

Precariat Poor people whose standard of living is precarious – who live, for instance, in the situation where a small financial setback will mean that they are unable to pay their rent, buy food, etc.

Rationing Sharing out food equally during times of shortage so that supplies can last longer.

Right-wing A political point of view that sees social inequality as inevitable, and typically promotes traditional social values. 'Hard right' politicians are more extreme in their views than the 'moderate right' or 'centre right' (terms that might be used of Britain's Conservative Party).

Segregate To be kept separate from others.

Slav A member of the people who live in East Europe and speak Slavic languages.

Sonderkommandos Jewish camp inmates who operated the crematoria and other facilities in the death camps.

Superpower A term used to describe a country or empire that is pre-eminent in its time – e.g. the USA and the USSR in the twentieth century.

Trenches A long, narrow ditch.

U-boat The German word for a submarine.

Utility housing Basic, often prefabricated ('prefab') houses, mass-built by the government or housing societies.

Variegated Widely different.

Wall Street Crash The name given to the collapse of the selling price of US stock market shares, 29 October 1929.

Footnote from page 11

While historian Richard Evans says Serbia bore the greatest responsibility, he goes on to say: 'Austria-Hungary bore only slightly less responsibility for its panic over-reaction to the assassination of the heir to the Habsburg throne. France encouraged Russia's aggressiveness towards Austria-Hungary and Germany encouraged Austrian intransigence. ... It is very important to look at the outbreak of the war in the round.

Answers to 'Think' on page 79:

A – Throwing eggs, B – Shouting, C – Raised fist, D – Communist hammer and sickle flag, E – Men and women of all races, and all ages, F – A 'Shall Not Pass' banner, G – A 'Shall Not Pass' hand gesture, H – Throwing leaflets I – A barricade made of furniture and an overturned car, J – Throwing ball bearings under horses' hooves, K – Police hitting out with truncheons, L – Police on horseback.

Answers to Enquiry Step 3 on page 112:

Dictatorship (A, D, E, F, G), Socialist Dream (B, C, D).

Index